KU-589-614

14. OCT 03

THE Corporate IMAGE

THE
Corporate
IMAGE

Strategies for
effective identity programmes

REVISED EDITION

Nicholas Ind

KOGAN
PAGE

First published in 1990
Revised edition published in 1992

Kogan Page Ltd
120 Pentonville Road
London N1 9JN

© Nicholas Ind, 1990, 1992

British Library Cataloguing in Publication Data

A CIP record for this book is available from the British Library.

ISBN 0–7494–0768–9 ✓

Typeset by J&L Composition Ltd, Filey, North Yorkshire
Printed and bound in Great Britain by
Biddles Ltd, Guildford and Kings Lynn

CONTENTS

LIST OF PLATES

LIST OF FIGURES

PREFACE

The raw material for the original version of this book was derived from desk research and interviews with UK and US based managers who had undertaken identity programmes and identity consultants. This was supplemented by the practical experience of researching, developing and implementing corporate identity programmes for a variety of organizations.

My contention, when I originally started work on the book in 1988 was that in spite of the increasing prominence of corporate identity as a business issue, there was nothing really written on the subject from a strategic viewpoint. Four years on and that thought still holds true. It remains an under-researched and somewhat confused area. As evidence for this, it is interesting to note that a 1991 study by the corporate identity consultancy Henrion Ludlow and Schmidt, and researcher MORI, into international attitudes towards corporate identity found a wide variance in attitudes towards the subject. Chris Ludlow, comparing the results to a 1989 study was moved to note:

> 'What's still remarkable is the extent to which people agree on the importance of corporate identity yet differ in their definition of what it is. It's almost as if corporate identity is something that fills a vacuum.'[1]

Perhaps most disappointing is the study's finding that British businessmen still strongly connect corporate identity with 'logos and design' – something which this book takes a stance against. Indeed the book, on the evidence of primary research, suggests that the most relevant and useful way to look at corporate identity is as something that affects and is affected by everything an organization says and does. None of the corporate identity projects I have undertaken since the first edition have suggested otherwise.

What has changed since 1989/90 is the economic climate. Now, we are in the depths of a recession. Two and a half years ago there was significant merger and acquisition activity, leveraged buy-outs and expansionism. The confidence of the business community was reflected in what I wrote. Although we will return at some point to an optimistic view, I have tried to temper this optimism, in this updated version of the book. I have also found it necessary to update some of the examples I originally used – not least because some such as British and Commonwealth and British Satellite Broadcasting have disappeared, but also because there are more recent and more relevant cases.

None of these amendments, however, have changed the basic message of the book: 'that corporate identity – properly understood and used – has a real part to play in competitive success.' Hopefully this new edition will help provide the wherewithal to make that happen.

Nicholas Ind
April 1992

References

[1] Marion Hancock, 'The Soul of a Company' *Design* (January 1992)

ACKNOWLEDGEMENTS

I would like to thank a number of people who helped in the development of the original edition and this revised version: Dr Jim Taggart who supervised my MBA study on corporate identity, John Ind for his advice on structure, Peter Spalding for help with research techniques, Feona McEwan for her reviews and comments and all those interviewees who provided me with information and support, especially Jeanette Lerman of Unisys, Jill Gabbe of Lippincott & Margulies, Amanda Haddon-Cave of Courtaulds, Wendy Millard of 3i, Flavio Gomez, David Canaan, Bob Seiler and Donata Maggipinto of SBG.

INTRODUCTION

The aim of this book is to explore the relationship between corporate identity and corporate strategy or, more precisely, to determine how a corporate identity can help a company to gain and sustain competitive advantage. The rationale behind this is that corporate identity or image (the problem of definition is discussed in Chapter 1) is perceived to be of increasing importance — witness the recent MORI survey which showed that 77 per cent of leading industrialists believe that the importance their company attaches to developing and promoting its corporate image will increase over the next few years.[1] However, the literature on the subject is sparse and, such as there is, is anecdotal. As yet, there seems to have been no systematic analysis of the way corporate identity works or is managed.

The brief to create a book that would be relevant in a practical way to both the corporate identity consultant and to corporate communications and marketing personnel, really determined the nature of the research and the structuring of the contents.

The research comprised extensive desk study, not primarily of design literature, but of books and articles on strategic management. Once I had completed this phase, I conducted in-depth interviews with design consultancies, companies (some of whom had undergone corporate identity reviews) and other authorities. The interviews, lasting anything from one hour to one day, were recorded and converted into transcripts, and form the basis of the analysis. The nature of the interviews often surprised the interviewees, because of the focus on corporate strategy and corporate communications in its broadest sense. This surprise was based on a belief that corporate identity was solely concerned with design issues. The seeming confusion about terminology also helped steer the structure of the book.

Part I provides precise definitions of the different terms used by consultants and companies. This in itself creates a problem, because when quoting interviewees or book sources the terms may be used in different ways. However, I believe that the context within which the quotes are placed will help to ensure clarity. In Chapter 2 we look at those factors in the overall economic environment that are making corporate identity a much discussed subject.

Part II shows how the three terms defined in Part I — identity, image and communication — are analysed. Throughout this section identity and strategy are constantly inter-related. Having completed what can often be a lengthy process, the communication and organizational problems of an organization would be defined.

Part III builds on the analysis of Part II to formulate the objectives of an identity programme and how they would be addressed, both in terms of design and also wider programmes of communication. This section thus sets design in context, and defines both its strengths and its limitations.

Part IV deals with one of the oft-forgotten aspects of an identity programme, that of making it work. Implementation planning, implementation and then the ongoing maintenance and ownership of an identity are discussed in turn. Finally, in Chapter 13, the means of evaluating an identity programme are discussed. Although this chapter recognizes the difficulty of clear evaluation, it also makes clear the importance of accountability.

References

[1] Market and Opinion Research International (MORI), *Study of Attitudes of Chairmen, Managing Directors and Other Mainboard Directors of Britain's 500 Largest Companies* (MORI, 1989)

PART I
AN INTRODUCTION TO
CORPORATE IDENTITY

If companies have always had identities and created images, why has it taken so long for 'corporate identity' to become established as a discipline in its own right? Part of the reason is that the very idea of marketing companies and products is relatively new. As a concept marketing only arrived in the UK by way of Procter and Gamble in the late 1950s and was originally focused very much on brands. However, in the last twenty years companies have begun to see the potential of marketing themselves; of communicating what they do and how they do it. None the less, even today some companies are only just coming to terms with the idea. For example, the British companies, BAT and Allied Breweries only discovered the need to communicate the extent of their activities when they came under threat of a takeover. Until they began to add their names to their brand advertising and started running corporate advertising compaigns as a defence mechanism, they had never bothered to project themselves corporately.

The second and equally strong reason for the slow acceptance of 'corporate identity' has been a real confusion as to what the term really means. In one sense 'corporate identity' has been in existence since the manufacturers of packaged goods began to use marks and typefaces to identify their brands and subsequently their companies. This type of 'identity' is firmly rooted in the world of graphic design and its modern form really goes back to the 1930s and 1940s, when designer Raymond Loewy created the International Harvester symbol and Edward Johnston developed graphics for the London Underground. However, in the 1960s, when the phrase 'corporate identity' was purportedly first coined by Walter Margulies, a New York-based design consultant, a new idea of the role of design in business began to emerge. Design consultancies such as Lippincott & Margulies in the US and Wolff Olins in the UK began to develop an approach that put the organization and its strategies first. The design of a corporate mark was not seen as an end in itself, but rather as an expression of the corporate strategy. This new and very different idea of corporate identity has existed side by side with the purely graphic idea of identity, and has managed to create considerable confusion, both in the business community and among the media. This has hindered the development of the more strategically orientated consultancies and the acceptance of corporate identity as anything more than just the creation of logos.

Now, in spite of the continued misinterpretation of the term, the pace of change in the business environment is such that companies have begun to be more aware of their corporate identity and the way in which they communicate it both to their employees and to their external audiences. Consequently, the strategic interpretation of corporate identity has begun to be recognized.

1

DEFINITIONS

Because the term 'corporate identity' has been used to describe two very different disciplines, companies enlisting the services of a corporate identity consultancy (or strategic design consultancy or design consultancy) are often unsure exactly what they are buying. To confuse the issue still further, some consultancies use terms like corporate identity, corporate image and corporate communication as if they are simply variants of the same concept. In order to clarify the meanings of these terms and reduce the amount of confusion, this chapter will provide precise definitions of each in turn.

'Corporate Identity'

Corporate identity is the term most commonly used to define the programme of communication and change that a company undertakes in conjunction with an external consultancy. In reality the term is a far more precise descriptor. An organization's identity is its *sense of self* — much like our own individual sense of identity. Consequently, it is unique. Identity is formed by an organization's history, its beliefs and philosophy, the nature of its technology, its ownership, its people, the personality of its leaders, its ethical and cultural values and its strategies. It can be projected or communicated through corporate identity programmes, but identity *per se* is very difficult to change. It is not something cosmetic, but is the core of an organization's existence. Successful and well-established companies like ICI and IBM have distinctive identities borne out of long- and widely-held beliefs and values. In his book on IBM, David Mercer notes that the beliefs of the modern founder of the company, Thomas J Watson, created a ubiquitous culture which is the very essence of the company's success even today:

> The one common factor that holds IBM together in a very rapidly changing world is not its technology, but its unique ethics and culture. It cannot be stressed too strongly just how important are the beliefs as the main driving force of IBM, as they will be for other companies seeking to emulate its particular style of management.[1]

If one accepts this idea of identity, most corporate identity programmes have to be seen as evolutionary, rather than as propagators of radical change. Philosophies and beliefs do not change overnight (in IBM they have not changed in over 50 years). Neither do identities. Such an event as suffered by ICI in the second half of 1980 when it recorded its first post-war loss, and cut dividends for the the first time in its history, can lead such a company to question its sense of identity and to re-orient itself. But even then ICI's core values proved resilient to change. If we look at the 'new World Class' ICI we see a company which is successful, clearly structured and has a clear strategic direction. None the less it is unquestionably ICI — the strategy may be more weighted to added-value products, but the identity of the company has not changed in any fundamental sense. As Nick Townsend of design consultants Landor Associates notes about ICI's revised logo: 'It wasn't a question of trying to signal radical change. It was a question of symbolizing that the company was evolving, that the good things about ICI are still there, but it's now more modern.'

Corporate trauma and identity

However, when a company suffers a real corporate trauma, such as a takeover, government intervention or significant down-scaling, there is evidence to suggest that the company and its identity can become changed in a more fundamental way. AT&T, as a result of the 1984 break-up of its monopoly of the US telecommunications market, went through this type of trauma. It changed from a traditional, paternalistic, slow-moving corporation to a responsive and customer-oriented structure. Measures such as staffing reductions, acquisitions and international joint ventures all helped to change in a radical way what was once described as the most entrenched corporate culture in America. The orientation of the company has been forced to change to such an extent that its identity has also been transformed. However, even in this instance the change in the identity was not effected immediately, and the company still retains elements of the old culture.

Similarly, when International Harvester — with its Raymond Loewy-designed symbol and 150 year heritage — was sold to Tenneco, the company ceased being a loss making manufacturer of farm machinery and became a profitable truck manufacturer. The old International Harvester, in spite of the strength of its corporate name, was bureaucratic, paternalistic and non-innovative. With a change in the nature of the business, a shift in focus away from controlling a million dollar a day loss to building a profitable organization and the setting of new corporate goals, the company began to acquire a distinctively different new identity.

'Corporate Image'

Corporate image is in the eye of the receiver. An organization may transmit a message about itself to its employees, its investors, its customers, and all its internal and external audiences. It may indeed wish to convey a particular self image, but it is the *reception* of the message that is the important factor. The corporate image is simply the picture that an audience has of an organization through the accumulation of all received messages. An organization may commonly assume that it only communicates when it wants to, but in reality it communicates through everything it says and does.

Both intentional and unintentional messages get through to audiences all the time, undermining those forms of communication that are more controllable, such as advertising and PR campaigns designed to create the right sort of picture of the organization. In this context the 'right' picture is an image that helps rather than hinders the achievement of the corporate strategy. The inescapable conclusion is that creating the right image is a never-ending and all-encompassing task. It is not simply about the creation of a corporate logo, it is a commitment to a corporate lifestyle.

It is important to remember that whereas a brand has a limited number of audiences, the company itself has many. These audiences include groups such as union officials, customers, suppliers, shareholders, market analysts and employees who sometimes have conflicting expectations of an organization. For example, an advertisement placed in the *Financial Times* to announce a massive rise in British Telecom's profits will be welcome news to its loyal shareholders who will then see the company as well run and efficient. However, the perception of the telephone user and the telecom unions may be entirely different. The telephone user may see windfall profits being derived from excessive charges, while the unions may see profits as a rationale for wage increases for their members. The political allegiances of these groups and whether they were pro- or anti-privatization in the first place will further colour their perceptions as to whether or not British Telecom is a 'good' company.

International images

Once we enter the field of international images, cultural differences create the problem of different interpretations of a message or symbol. Although many post-war writers have noted that cultures seem to have become more alike, there are still sufficient cultural peculiarities to inhibit and distort meaning. For example, in spite of the brutalities of the Second World War, Cretans still paint swastikas on their homes as a good luck symbol. To other Europeans who associate the swastika with the Nazi regime and its repression, the symbol seems incongruous.

Another example of differing cultural viewpoints comes from Mankiewicz's film *Julius Caesar*. Roland Barthes, in his essay on the picture entitled 'The Romans in Films', points out that all the characters in Mankiewicz's film wear fringes as a demonstration of their 'Romanness'. This signifier may work with American audiences, but it fails with the French:

A Frenchman to whose eyes American faces still have some-thing exotic, finds comical the combination of the morphologies of these gangster sheriffs with the little Roman fringe: it looks like an excellent music-hall gag. This is because for the French the sign in this case overshoots the target and discredits itself by letting its aim appear clearly.[2]

What these examples imply is that an international organization must use symbols that convey a consistent message, otherwise its intentions may be misinterpreted. In order to do this companies have to understand the nature of their international audiences, their cultural values and their motivations.

The unwanted image

Unlike identity, image is relatively transmutable. Although it may require a concerted effort to change an entrenched image, perceptions of an organization can be formed quickly. Conversely, a previously positive image can be transformed into a negative one with frightening rapidity.

In the 1980s Ratners plc transformed itself from a thriving UK jewellery store chain into a dominant international group. However, in so doing it did not change its strategy. Whatever the retail trading name the focus was on providing good value jewellery products to a mass market. The City applauded this no-nonsense strategy. Then in April 1991, Chief Executive, Gerald Ratner made a speech at the Institute of Directors in London and referred to his company's products as 'crap'. The reference was picked up by the national press and turned into an issue. Not only was the remark seen as personally injudicious, leading Gerald Ratner to bring in a new Chairman, but there was much comment as to whether the Ratners brand name had acquired such negative connotations that it would have to be dropped. Nothing had changed with the *tangible* product, but the *intangible* image was tarnished.

Similarly, Lonrho, a UK-based conglomerate was transformed from a little-known company into 'the unacceptable face of capitalism' by the then Conservative Prime Minister, Edward Heath. Whatever the reality of the company's activities, the tag has stuck, and was used again by a Labour MP when Lonrho took its first stake in Harrods.

In contrast, the power of a strong and positive image such as

Shell, the Anglo-Dutch oil company, has built up through a concerted PR and advertising campaign can help overcome the negative. When the company was responsible for a major oil spillage in the River Mersey in 1989 it was criticized widely in the press. However, the rapid response to clean up the pollution and the company's environmentally friendly image meant the damage to the company's reputation, although deep, was short lived. Of course, if Shell continued to create oil spillages then the image would become negative and long term — a situation that would be difficult to correct.

✳'Corporate Communication'

Corporate communication is the process that translates an identity into an image. This is a vital part of the process because a corporate identity, if it is to have any value, has to be communicated to employees, shareholders and customers alike. Without communication the values and strategies of the organization will not be understood or owned and the company will not have any clear sense of identity. For example, IBM's identity is particularly pervasive because its beliefs are 'widely held'. This suggests that communication cannot just be defined in the narrow sense of the word. It is more than just advertising and PR. It is everything a company does from the way that telephones are answered to the way product brochures are presented. As Wally Olins of Wolff Olins says: 'The fundamental idea behind a corporate identity programme is that in everything a company does, everything it owns, everything it produces, the company should project a clear idea of what it is and what its aims are.'[3]

The logo

The development of a design system, or a corporate mark or logo, is thus only a part of the means of communicating with a company's audiences. The design process has the important role of creating the visual statement which will signify what a company stands for and it has the function of providing a focus for the managers and employees of a company and of communicating a consistent message to customers, financial analysts and suppliers.

None the less, the logo is only a symbol, and we should be wary about ascribing too much value to it. The designer Rodney Fitch notes: 'The alternative to a new board of directors is not some new stationery and a logo.'

A logo, as with many graphic symbols, has limited significance in its own right. First, as we have seen, the cultural background of the audience will determine the interpretation. Writers, such as Kenichi Ohmae in his book *Triad Power* see these cultural quirks disappearing in a rapidly homogenizing world, but graphic symbols or even typefaces which rely on an understanding of a particular cultural history for their relevance will still tend to be lost on other cultures.[4]

The second factor that limits the power of the logo is that a corporate symbol must always be related to a context. For example, the symbol of Diana, used by the book publishers, Bloomsbury (Plate 1), has a meaning that is independent of the company. In the context of classical mythology Diana is the goddess of hunting and midwifery. Bloomsbury chose the graphic device because the idea of hunting out authors and then bringing works to life seemed appropriate connotations for a publisher. More practically, Diana's bow could be bent into a 'B' to represent the company name. Whether or not the company's readers know what Diana stands for matters little in this instance. Over time the picture of Diana and Bloomsbury, the quality of their products and the company's performance will become inseparable. Thus, a corporate mark or logo does not have an independent reality of its own, but it is related to the experience and the expectations of the audience.

Of course, if a company wants to be thought of as having specific attributes, such as being large and efficient, that image can be created by using imagery suggesting size and efficiency. However, if the company singularly *fails* to be large and efficient a gap will open up between perception and reality. Corporate communication is not a panacea. It will not turn a poor company into a success. What it *can* do is convey a consistent and credible message of what a company is, what it does, and how it does it, by trying to control the messages it transmits. Where those messages contradict each other the overall image of the company will tend to be confused. The corollary of this is that corporate communications require not only analysis, but also good management.

Corporate Identity Programmes

The management of an organization's identity falls very much upon the shoulders of senior managers. Only they can reinforce an existing strong identity or help to change a poor one. The role of the consultant and the nature of 'corporate identity programmes' is quite specific. The identity consultant is employed to create a system, a sense of order in the communications process, that reflects the company's identity in creating a corporate image which helps achieve the corporate strategy.

Two points are worth noting about this. Firstly, the system that the identity consultant creates should steer all overt communications, by sitting above the company's PR and advertising and design strategies and determining the way a company is presented, whatever the media used. Only then can consistency of communication be created.

Secondly, it must be remembered that the most important audience and communicators in any company are the employees. As an audience their perceptions of the organization will in no small measure determine their attitudes and behaviour, which will in turn affect the way in which they communicate with the outside world in their everyday dealings. To change attitudes and behaviour of employees takes a consistent and concerted effort, which starts by changing perceptions. Thus, communicating with employees is a vital prerequisite in any programme of change. However, it is not enough. Communication programmes need to be accompanied by other programmes of training and inter-action, if lasting and effective change is to be achieved. Although a consultancy may recommend and support these other programmes, the onus is on the client company to implement them. This underlines both the strengths and the limitations of identity programmes. Nick Townsend of Landor Associates supports this specific definition of identity programmes:

Corporate identity is a powerful tool in the corporate tool kit, which enables you to communicate change; it enables you to communicate direction and it enables you to communicate your point of difference. And why that is valuable is because of everything you do in business, communications is probably the hardest thing.

Summary

The three definitions can be summarized as follows:

1. *Corporate identity* is the accumulation of a company's history and its strategies. It is not easily changed. Most identities evolve gradually over time, but a significant event such as a takeover can change the identity radically.

2. A *corporate image* is the picture a company's audiences have of it. It will be determined by all a company's actions. The problem a company faces is that different audiences will interpret a message in different ways. The management of the corporate image is thus an ongoing task.

3. *Corporate communication* is the process that translates corporate identity into a corporate image. The identity needs to be communicated to employees, customers and shareholders if it is to have any value. The role of design within this is to visually signify what a company stands for.

References

[1] David Mercer, *IBM: How the World's Most Successful Corporation is Managed* (Kogan Page, 1987) p 240
[2] Roland Barthes, *Mythologies* (Paladin, 1973) p 27/28
[3] Wally Olins, *The Wolff Olins Guide to Corporate Identity* (1984)
[4] Kenichi Ohmae, *Triad Power: The Coming Shape of Global Competition* (The Free Press, 1985)

2

THE VALUE OF CORPORATE IDENTITY

With the first oil crisis of 1973, the business environment moved from a period of relative stability to one of flux. The pace of change has kept going and has placed pressure on companies continually to review the way they do business. Globalization, corporate raiders and leveraged buyouts, government deregulation, privatizations and recession, have all forced companies to re-orient and re-position themselves in their markets. They have had to look to their identities and determine whether they remain relevant in the light of change. In this chapter we will examine the changes in the environment that have caused corporate identity programmes to become more widely valued.

The Acceleration of Product Life Cycles

The theory of the product life cycle is that there is a natural evolution for products from their introduction through to their growth, maturity and eventual decline. While the life cycle is not really valid as a means of predicting an industry's evolution, not least because industry participants can affect the outcome, it does have value in describing how an industry is evolving. The traditional picture of the life cycle shows a slow transition from product launch through consumer trial to growing consumer acceptance and the introduction of substitute products culminating in slowly diminishing sales. Even the shape of the product life cycle is a lazy wave suggesting longevity (Figure 1). For many

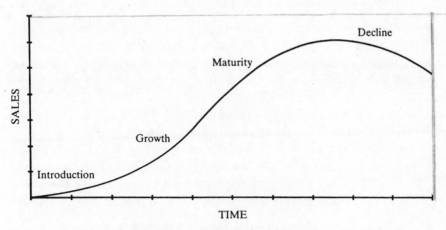

Figure 1   A product life cycle

industries, especially those with a long heritage, this picture still holds true.

However, the process has begun to break down over the last decade and many product life cycles are no longer the lazy curve. The wave is now a steep-sided line. The introduction of computers, the more rapid diffusion of technology, more flexible manufacturing processes, and the demands of consumers have all contributed to the acceleration of life cycles. Products might gain acceptance more easily, but often their decline is just as rapid.

Nowhere is this more in evidence than in the audio market. In fairly rapid succession, tapes have displaced records and compact discs have displaced tapes. Similarly, in audio hardware, tower systems have displaced music centres, midi systems have displaced towers, midis have been overtaken by minis, and in the future everything will probably be replaced by integrated communication systems. Some find this pace of change unnerving. In the search for the new there is an inevitable element of insecurity created, but this is part of the price to be paid in meeting consumers' ever-changing demands.

From a corporate perspective this increasing rate of change leads to certain conclusions.

- Firstly, corporate structures need to be geared up for change. Organizations need to respond faster to shifts in consumer attitudes and behaviour and they need to respond with purpose.

- Secondly, as markets are evolving with increasing rapidity, the companies that serve those markets have to assess their market positions continually in case they become untenable. If a move has to be effected then companies have to re-orient themselves to their relevant audiences. In the more radical cases it may mean an acquisition or merger in order to survive. However, in most instances, as an industry changes, companies simply outgrow their previous positions and they look to new markets or new products to fuel future growth. Thus, Ford now gets something like a third of its profits from its finance business, and USX, once purely a steel company, is now an oil producer.

- Thirdly, given the potential for uncertainty in new markets, a strong corporate brand name with sufficient flexibility to be applied to a variety of products, will give a company a head start. For example, such is the strength of Sony as a corporate brand that it has the potential to be applied to TVs, cameras, audio systems, videos and computers. With each new product launch the Sony name adds value and reduces uncertainty for both distributors and customers.

The Difficulty of Differentiation

Many companies would argue that it has always been difficult to find a way of standing out from one's competitors and probably still more would argue that maintaining the differentiation is doubly difficult. If this were true in the past, it is certainly true now. Of course, one could question whether trying to be different is really worthwhile. If a formula works for one company, why shouldn't it work for the next? In many respects it will. There is a certain sameness in much of clothes retailing, caused by a tendency to follow rather than innovate.

However, consumers want choice, and the company that offers something that is relevantly different, either in the form of pricing, or its distinctive products, will have an advantage over its competitors. Also, as Michael Porter, the author of *Competitive Advantage* and *Competitive Strategy*, has cogently argued, because each individual firm interacts in a different way with the forces that drive industry competition it will have a different optimal position: 'Competitive strategy involves positioning a business to maximize the value of the capabilities that distinguish it from its competitors.'[1]

If we accept the benefits of differentiation, the next task is to find the means to be different. The problem is that in many industries it is difficult to sustain a real point of difference. In financial services, for example, certain factors are taken as pre-requisites. A product has to have a competitive rate of interest, an acceptable degree of flexibility and a certain level of security. The relative weight of these areas will vary depending on the nature of the product, but if the balance of these factors is not right, the product will not even make the consumer's 'shopping list'.

Most financial service companies offer a range of products that are a trade-off between interest paid, flexibility and security. This, and the ease with which products can be copied tends to create a certain sameness about most financial offerings. As Alan Goy of Midland Bank has said: 'There is nothing unique about a financial services product.'

The means by which consumers discriminate between one product and another tend to be emotional rather than purely rational. It is the perception of past performance, the quality of service and the expectations of the customer that provide the basis of differentiation. The element of added value is the presentation of a clear and relevant identity to the consumer. Notably, bank advertising concentrates on creating an image based around these service messages, with TSB's 'Bank that likes to say Yes' and Midland's 'The Listening Bank' being two of the more consistent themes.

For corporate identity consultants, the financial services sector has become a key area of business. Companies have discovered that they have to communicate their services as if they were branded products in order to convey a cohesive image. The Prudential, a well-established life assurance company with a history stretching back over 140 years, has developed a new corporate symbol (Plate 2) based on the figure of Prudence (who represents wise conduct — one of the cardinal virtues), which is used on all the company's communications. It is a sign to all audiences of the value and security of Prudential products. It creates an expectation that the life assurance product one buys from the company will perform to the same standards as the pension product. The parallel with branded goods is obvious. It is just the same when we purchase a tin of Heinz baked beans. Previous experience of the product means that a Heinz label creates an expectation of a certain level of quality from the next purchase.

Differentiation and manufactured goods

The problems of differentiation also apply to manufactured goods. Although new industries tend to provide differentiated products at first, over time those differences become dissipated. Michael Porter cites a number of reasons why this should happen. Firstly, through repeat purchase, buyers start to learn about a product's performance and that of its competitors:

> Products have a tendency to become more like commodities over time as buyers become more sophisticated and purchasing tends to be based on better information. Thus there is a natural force reducing product differentiation over time in an industry.[2]

Secondly, consumer uncertainties over technology or performance tend to be resolved. New industries often take time to prove themselves and to overcome buyer inertia and technological problems. The battle for the UK satellite TV market is a case in point. Originally there were two competitive and incompatible technologies on offer. British Satellite Broadcasting (BSB) with its square satellite dish and Sky Television with its round dish. BSB in particular suffered from technical problems with dish production, which gave Sky the opportunity to launch first. However, consumer take up was slow, partly because it was unclear which was the best format and pundits were predicting that only one technology would survive. With both companies investing huge development sums, something had to give. Having only achieved sales of 150,000 'squarials' and losing large sums of money, BSB's consortium of backers decided to sell and in November 1990 BSB was merged with Sky to form another BSB: British Sky Broadcasting based on Sky's round dish technology. One key element of product differentiation — the dish — thus disappeared.

A similar and well-documented case of disappearing product differentiation is the video cassette recorder (VCR) market. At the outset there were three competing technologies, Philips' V2000 system, Sony's Betamax and JVC's VHS. Initially the market was able to accommodate all three technologies, but of these now only VHS survives, with both Sony and Philips using this operating format.

Manufacturers no longer compete on the relative merits of their respective technologies, but on features, design and image. The lesson to be learnt from the VCR market is that the protection of technology by patents and proprietary knowledge can be counter-productive. It is generally held that VHS was technologically inferior, but because JVC provided the technology to other manufacturers it gained the best penetration and became the standard format. The original basis of differentiation disappeared in the VCR industry within the space of a few years. Porter notes that whatever the technological strategy of a company, there is a tendency for both product and process technology to become less proprietary as an industry develops. Battlegrounds shift as knowledge becomes more established and widespread.

The tendency towards product and corporate sameness means that companies have to maximize the potential of their unique attributes, and ensure that they are communicated to the relevant audiences. Even when a company is able to differentiate itself, it then has to communicate the fact to the purchasers of its products. And the factors of differentiation have to *matter* to buyers. They must have the potential to be discriminators, not just motivators. It is no good creating an image of a technologically advanced company, if technology is irrelevant to buyers. Nor is it useful to attempt to create an image of an efficient, well-run company, when you are not. This is the view of corporate identity as a cosmetic device. It is only useful to communicate a real point of differentiation.

The Pull of Decentralization

The continued move towards globalization in many industries has been accompanied by the principle of decentralization. The rationale behind a decentralized organization is that it is closer to the needs of the market, and the management are easier to motivate because they enjoy greater autonomy. This is the rationale behind the 'think global, act local' dictum of many multinationals.

However, it can cause potential problems for the identity of an organization. Autonomous operations are likely to develop identities of their own which may run counter to the needs of the parent organization. The following examples demonstrate both the positives and negatives of decentralization and the implications for identities.

Hillsdown Holdings

Hillsdown Holdings is one of the largest businesses in the UK, with a 1991 turnover of £4.5 billion. It is also one of the least well known. The company is the country's biggest egg packer, chicken processor and meat producer, but retains its anonymity by using the individual company names within the group, rather than its own. Each of the 200 subsidiaries it owns throughout the world has retained its own identity, and is largely autonomous: 'The only form of central control is financial. Every month, the managing director of each subsidiary submits a two page report to head office. As well as covering the month's events and performance, he is expected and trusted, to include any bad news.'[3]

Hillsdown has made no attempt to impose its own visual identity on the component parts of the group. Indeed, the retention of some strong brand names such as Buxted Chicken, Lockwoods tinned foods and Christie-Tyler furniture, is part of the group's strength.

However, there are penalties for this approach. Firstly, there is virtually no horizontal communication in the group, so any potential for synergy is ignored and secondly, Hillsdown's deliberately low profile has tended to cause shareholder disinterest.

Against this are the high levels of motivation within the individual operating companies, and although there is no cohesive visual identity for the group, there is a collective identity based on entrepreneurship and a commitment to performance. There seems to be a consistent set of beliefs held by the operational managers which pulls the component parts into a group.

Globally-oriented Companies

Within globally-oriented companies it seems that the level of decentralization varies. A 1985 study by Young, Hood and Hamill of 154 UK-based subsidiaries of multinationals showed that finance and research and development were the most centralized; personnel the most decentralized. Production and marketing fell between these two extremes. The problem that most international companies face is to get the balance between centralized and decentralized operations right and to ensure there is cohesion between the operations.

Of course, these strictures would also apply equally well to nationally-oriented companies, but the geographical dispersion of international companies tends to exacerbate the problem.

Courtaulds

The UK-based Courtaulds group has geographically dispersed activities in no less than six business areas: fibres; woodpulp; chemicals and materials; coatings; films and packaging; and textiles. (Courtaulds Textiles has recently been floated as a separate organization.) However, the company considers itself to be a group rather than a conglomerate, because each one of these sectors is related to at least one other. This group view is in part endorsed by the co-operation across business areas in new product work such as the development of carbon fibre:

> Much of the pioneering work in the development of carbon fibre has been carried out by the British Courtaulds Group, who have brought together fibre expertise, polymer knowledge and weaving skills from their different divisions to develop a material of remarkable versatility.[4]

Not only does there have to be a system to stimulate the cross-referral of ideas, but there also has to be a sense of collective identity and communication across corporate structures. For Courtaulds, the combination of diverse product groups and dispersed geographical operations makes this especially difficult. Until the latest corporate identity review was undertaken, the practice of allowing operating companies to use their traditional names made it doubly so and led to incongruities, such as two

Courtaulds companies in the same country being unaware that they were part of the same group. The new identity system aims to correct this lack of group cohesion by a common naming policy. Now, everything is branded Courtaulds. The implication is that while overseas subsidiaries have to be given a certain level of control over their own destiny, there also needs to be co-ordination from the centre. To achieve this and to balance the pull of decentralization, there have to be countervailing forces. A well-communicated group-wide identity is one means of achieving this.

Department for Enterprise

We do not have to use a global organization to demonstrate the pull of decentralization. To communicate its positioning as the Department for Enterprise, the Department of Trade and Industry has gone through the process of developing a new visual identity system. This not only implies a more entrepreneurial organization, but also greater levels of decentralization. 'The whole emphasis on improved management within the Civil Service under the Thatcher administration has been increased decentralization.'

The Department of Trade and Industry has tried to counter-balance decentralization by introducing a naming policy that draws together the Department's disparate operations under the umbrella of DTI — the Department for Enterprise (Plate 3). To ensure that the new programme works in practice, central control of all visual communication has been strengthened.

A set of shared values and the communication of those values through identity programmes can help to balance the pressures of decentralization and stimulate greater levels of co-ordination. Although the degree of decentralization among companies varies, the increasing globalization of many industries will only help to stimulate further decentralization, as the only practical response to the increased scale of operations.

Changing Patterns of Competition

It is rather clichéd to claim that the nature of competition is changing. However, over the last five years the Japanese have forced Western companies out of their complacency; companies have expanded rapidly through mergers and acquisitions and then contracted again to reduce levels of debt; conglomerates have largely disappeared and been replaced by focused groups; markets have become more concentrated; companies and their brands have become more globalized and governments everywhere have been stepping back and either encouraging or even forcing companies into free market competition. Implicit in all this change is the need for the organization to redefine its purpose and its communications to both internal and external audiences.

Mergers and Acquisitions

A merger or acquisition inevitably leads to an assessment of an organization's actual identity. Indeed, an organization's profile can be radically altered. After an acquisition management start to ask 'Who are we? What business are we in?' After the deal is ratified by the shareholders such questions have to be answered by an analytical process that aims to determine the strengths and the weaknesses of the respective companies prior to the merger, and the anticipated strengths and weaknesses of the unified company.

The result of this analysis may lead to re-evaluation of the various identities within the corporate portfolio. With the merger of two large multinationals it is not impossible for there to be 100 or more separate identities and each of these will have to be assessed to determine their strengths and whether or not they help fulfil group goals. This may have implications for the way the group is structured, and it will almost inevitably involve some renaming.

The core issue here will be to determine whether operating units need to be presented as part of the group, or disassociated from it. As with the Courtaulds example, a decision may be taken to rename everything under one name, or a company may decide to follow the Hillsdown route and play down any connection.

37

Divestments

The same arguments apply in the case of divestment. In the 1960s and early 1970s, many corporations went in for broadly based acquisitions, and often found themselves competing in industries in which they had little or no experience. Unless they could create some synergy from their acquisitions they were only duplicating what an ordinary shareholder could do by holding a portfolio of shares. In no sense were they creating shareholder value.

As competition intensified in the 1980s many organizations began to focus back towards what they know best and they have now re-worked their visual identities to signal this change. Companies like Transamerica, Unilever and Reed International have in the last few years reverted back to core activities and have sold off part of their businesses, either to outsiders, or through management buyouts. This latter form of divestment saw huge growth in the late eighties and was estimated to account for 14 per cent of all acquisitions in the UK in 1988.

A divestment will have implications for the identity of both the acquirers and the sellers. Potentially it can radically alter the profile of the selling group. In the 1980s, Saatchi and Saatchi plc attempted to move away from its advertising roots and become a world leader in consultancy and marketing services. To this end it acquired a variety of companies in design, market research, public relations, direct marketing and management consultancy. The latter spearheaded by the 1984 acquisition of the Washington based Hay group was an attempt to make Saatchi as big in consultancy as it was in advertising. However, in spite of a number of small and medium sized acquisitions, the consultancy business never lived up to expectations and by 1989 it was up for sale. Over the last three years Saatchi has re-worked its strategy, divested its 'peripheral' interests and focused back on its core strength: advertising. Although the company has come in for considerable criticism about its past foray into areas outside its perceived expertise, Robert Louis-Dreyfus, the company's Chief Executive, has worked hard to communicate the new focused positioning to financial audiences.

Similarly, when a management buyout team breaks away from a publicly-quoted organization, they normally do so in a fanfare of publicity. Thereafter the organization will often disappear from view. The necessity of communicating with market analysts, financial journalists and institutional investors is no longer important. There is no need to publish interim and full year accounts. Private ownership implies privacy for many companies. Also, the direct involvement of managers in a new venture is time consuming and involving, so communication may come low down on the list. There may be a sense of identity, and a set of shared values within the new organization, but the company may fail to create the kind of image it wants with its buyers, suppliers and backers. This may undermine the potential of the company, and it can certainly have implications if the company decides to enter public ownership at a later date.

Privatizations and Deregulation

Both the US and the UK have seen government intervention change the nature of competition. In the US this has taken the form of deregulation of industries, such as airlines and banking and the breakup of monopolies such at AT&T.

In the UK, it has been a matter of public policy under the Conservative administration to reduce the number of organizations controlled by the government. Since 1979, British Gas, British Airways, Jaguar, British Steel, British Telecom, and Rover Group have all been either sold to a third party or floated on the stock market.

The process of transition has not always been easy. All the British companies mentioned above have had to make the change from living with the vagaries of government control to a more market-oriented stance. In the past all nationalized industries were subject to the Public Sector Borrowing Requirement and had to fight for their share of public funds. Often this resulted in under-investment.

Consequently, when such companies, some of whom had enjoyed monopolies, were launched into a competitive world they found it difficult to achieve the performance levels expected of them. Both British Telecom and AT&T have had to learn to live with new corporate realities since their respective monopolies in telecom systems were taken away. Andrew Kupfer, writing in *Fortune*, notes of AT&T that:

The company could no longer operate as the regulated monopoly it once was, satisfied with predictable price increases, complacent about competition, uncritical of costs. To compete in fast changing markets — for that is where divestiture has taken all AT&T's businesses — the telephone company of old had to learn to get aggressive, to take chances and above all, to move quickly.[5]

The process of moving from one form of organization to another has proved difficult. It has necessitated a questioning of fundamental beliefs and a reappraisal of the corporate identity. To signal the organizational changes that AT&T was undergoing, the American designer, Saul Bass was appointed to develop a new logo style that could be implemented across all communications. The resultant graphic was a radical break with the past to reflect the radical changes in the organization and the move from a national telephone company to a worldwide telecommunications group.

A similar process of corporate reappraisal has taken place in the US, since the Airline Deregulation Act of 1978. The fear for airline deregulation at the time was that it would create a free-for-all, which at the end of the day would benefit no one. Deregulation still has its critics both in government and among users, but against most measurable parameters it has been a success. It is more questionable whether the quality of service has improved, but it would seem that in this respect the airlines have been victims of their ability to attract ever-increasing numbers of customers.

Deregulation, like privatization and divestiture, has caused much soul searching among the carriers themselves. The industry structure has changed significantly over the last decade. There has been an increasing concentration in the industry with the smaller airlines either being acquired or forced out of business. Now just four airlines dominate US air traffic. The consequence of this merger activity has been a continual reappraisal of corporate names and the means by which companies present their identities.

Globalization

Globalization is a fact of life in an increasing number of industries and is one of the key catalysts of corporate identity programmes. As companies begin to operate on an international basis, the image that they acquired as national producers often becomes inappropriate. For example, American Express used to be a nationally competitive freight company with an image that was related to its performance in this product field. This was singularly inappropriate when the organization developed into a global travel agent, credit card and banking company. As the identity of the company changed, so its communications changed with it.

Similarly, companies sometimes enter foreign markets through an acquisition, which creates the difficult situation of whether to retain the existing corporate brand and its goodwill, or to impose their global brand name. Often there is an element of jingoism about the encroachment of overseas companies into domestic markets and consequently the existing names are retained, at least in the short term. However, some companies do opt for a unified global brand in spite of the negative reactions of governments or consumers. For example, Renault Trucks acquired the Dodge brand in the UK from Peugeot. In the short term the company was anxious about relinquishing such a valuable company name, but in the end the company decided that a cohesive global identity was more important, so Dodge was replaced by Renault branding.

An ubiquitous corporate identity is a good means of encouraging coordination and cohesion, especially if the operations are globally dispersed. In an international context that means evolving an identity based on global strengths and perspectives. This does not necessarily mean a slavish adherence to a global corporate identity. The degree to which the identity is adapted to the host country culture will depend on the strength of that culture and whether competitive advantage is derived primarily from co-ordinating activities centrally or by devolving activities to operational markets. However, if the company has a true global orientation it will generally need to convey consistent values wherever it competes. Thus, the worldwide image that emerges is more likely to be notable for its homogeneity than not. The value of this is ever more enhanced as all corporate audiences become more travelled.

IBM's identity is truly international. It represents the same core values, wherever it is in the world. As long as competition continues to evolve internationally, and this can only continue to accelerate with European integration, the requirement for international corporate images that work across national boundaries will increase.

The Costs of Communication

In the UK, media inflation has consistently outstripped the retail price index and the media market place has become ever more crowded and expensive, putting pressure on all communicators to make cost-effective use of their promotional moneys. This has had two key implications for corporate identity:

- As the costs of communication have spiralled upwards, it has become ever more expensive to support a large number of brand names. One means of overcoming this pressure and achieving economic communication is either to reduce the number of brands supported, or to brand everything in a consistent way so that a message is conveyed more cost-effectively. Indeed, part of the reason for Renault Trucks deciding to discard the Dodge brand was that on limited budgets it was not viable to support two brand names.

- The search for media value has caused companies to rely less on conventional advertising to convey their message, and more on other forms of communication such as design, PR, sales promotion and direct marketing. Whereas 10 years ago promotional expenditure in the UK was 47 per cent of total advertising and promotional expenditure, it now accounts for over 55 per cent. The danger is that as companies appoint a variety of communication advisers, all of whom are using different media, the message that the company is sending out starts to become confused.

However, all the elements of a company's communication need to work together, whether the company is making an on-pack offer for one of its products or conducting a corporate advertising campaign. An overall tone needs to be set that determines the presentation of the company in its PR, advertising and design. This is the role of corporate identity programmes.

Summary

1. The business environment has been undergoing significant and rapid change over the last decade which has altered both the structure and direction of a large number of companies. To compete effectively companies have often had to review their identities and the way they communicate those identities to create an image that is relevant to the corporate strategy.

2. The acceleration of product life cycles has placed a continual pressure on companies to re-position themselves in their markets. Whereas a company's products used to evolve slowly, there is now a tendency for products to succeed very quickly and then die.

3. It is increasingly difficult for both service and manufacturing companies to differentiate themselves from each other. The communication of a distinctive corporate identity is one means of achieving a unique positioning for a company.

4. As companies grow larger, so their operations tend to become geographically more dispersed. As business units become separated away from the parent company there is a danger that they will start to present contradictory messages. One means of counteracting the pull of decentralization is the development of a common corporate identity to help weld an organization together.

5. Mergers, acquisitions, divestments, privatizations, deregulations and recession are changing the nature of competition in a radical way. These are the sort of events that can cause a corporate identity to undergo a profound change.

6. As more and more industries become globalized, so the organizations that compete in those industries have had to try to create identities that take account of their source of competitive advantage. This may involve the development of identities related to individual countries or the imposition of a global identity.

7. Communications are becoming ever more expensive, but economies of communication can be achieved by ensuring that a message is presented consistently, whatever the media.

References

[1] Michael Porter, *Competitive Strategy* (The Free Press, 1980) p 47
[2] Michael Porter, *Competitive Strategy* (The Free Press) p 170
[3] Chris Blackhurst, 'Leader of the Pack', *Business Magazine* (January 1989)
[4] *The Times* (8 July 1988)
[5] Andrew Kupfer 'Cover Story on AT&T' *Fortune International* (19 June 1989)

PART II
CORPORATE IDENTITY IN PRACTICE

The first two chapters of this book have been concerned with demonstrating the nature of corporate identity, and the factors within the overall business environment that have made corporate identity increasingly important to competitive success. In the next four chapters we will concentrate on showing how corporate identity programmes work in practice, from the initial investigative process through to defining the positioning of an organization as it really is, and as it is seen to be. These chapters follow in sequence the analytical model in Figure 2. The benefit of this model is that it takes us away from the purely visual notion of corporate identity and focuses our thinking on the inter-relationship between identity and strategy.

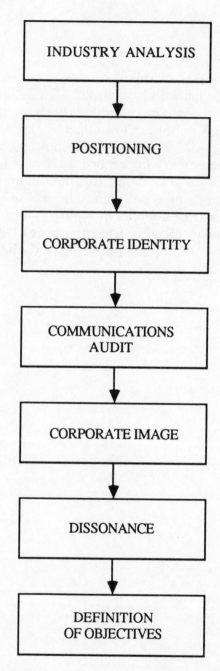

Figure 2   A strategic approach to corporate identity programmes

3

CORPORATE STRATEGY AND CORPORATE IDENTITY

We now need to develop a framework for analysing a strategic view of identity. This must start with an understanding of the way corporate identity inter-relates with strategy.

Corporate Strategy

Philip Kotler describes 'strategy' in the following terms:

> All companies must look beyond their present situation and develop a long-term strategy to meet changing conditions in their industry. They must develop a game plan for achieving their long run objectives. There is no one strategy that is optimal for all companies. Each company must determine what makes the most sense in the light of its position in the industry and its objectives, opportunities and resources.[1]

Four points can be extracted from this definition, all of which have implications for corporate identity:

- Corporate strategy takes a long term view of the changing nature of an industry.
- Each company is unique.
- Corporate strategy must be built on an understanding of a company's positioning.
- A company has to understand the nature of its resources.

However, before looking at these points in some detail, we need to understand in general terms the role of corporate identity in corporate strategy. This works in two ways. Firstly, the organization's identity will influence the setting of objectives and the determination of a strategy. In other words, what you are will affect your aims and how you set about achieving them. For example, if a company has grown up with a philosophy that believes in the autonomy of business units, the strategy will either have to accept the philosophy or try to change it. It cannot ignore it.

Secondly, the nature of the objectives set and the way the company goes about achieving them will impinge on the identity. To extend the previous example, if a company recognizes that the key to success in its market is strong central control of its resources, then the strategy must take this into account and look to reduce the autonomy of business units. This is then likely to affect the corporate belief in business unit autonomy.

The example of Turkiye Is Bankasi

Turkiye Is Bankasi is the leading bank in Turkey. Kemal Ataturk, the creator of modern Turkey, had been the founder and one of the major shareholders in the bank. The remaining shares in the organization had been held by employees and the government. On Ataturk's death his shares reverted to the state. As a consequence, the equity structure determined that a sizeable portion of the bank's income went to the Turkish treasury. Not surprisingly, with its central role in both corporate and personal finance, the bank's identity embodied Turkish national mores. Even today Ataturk's portrait hangs in each of the bank's 940 branches. However, banking has become increasingly competitive in Turkey and, with membership of the European Community imminent, the bank decided it needed to invest in updating its operations, which were often loss-making, by developing a new commitment to service and installing automated machinery in its branches.

With its heritage so closely linked to the Turkish economy, the company decided that its strategy had to be similar to that developed by Ataturk who used the bank to stimulate domestic finances after the revolution of 1919. It would therefore continue to provide domestic finance, while developing business internationally. This choice was fundamental to the future identity of the bank. In essence Turkiye Is Bankasi was to be a Turkish bank that carried on international business, rather than an international bank with a head office in Turkey. Having determined a strategic direction which was influenced by the historical identity of the bank, a more cohesive identity has itself been evolving in response to the strategic initiatives.

A Long-Term View

As an industry changes, so do corporate strategies and identities. Take for example Procter and Gamble (P&G). Traditionally P&G dominated the retail trade in the US, but consolidation of supermarkets and drugstores in the 1970s and 1980s shifted the balance of power to the retailers. P&G had to switch from a product-led strategy to a customer-led one. The impact of this has been to change the internal structure of the organization and the attitudes of staff. The strategic shift has brought about an evolution of the identity:

> Procter is taking the best of its past — a willingness to stay with long-term projects, job security, and a history of promotion from within — and grafting on to it a management style that calls for pushing authority down, speeding up decisions, and getting closer to the customer.[2]

However, a company cannot generally afford to wait until its industry changes to change its strategy. The strategy has to be forward looking and based upon a prediction of an industry's future evolution and the company's likely position within it. However, the process of analysis has to start with an understanding of the present.

The best available tool with which to conduct this initial analytical phase is Michael Porter's five forces model (Figure 3). This is concerned with five key areas, the relative strength of which determines the overall levels of profitability available within a specific industry. Porter argues that a company's ability to earn profits will be determined by its interaction with the five forces, but this will be constrained by the limitations of an industry

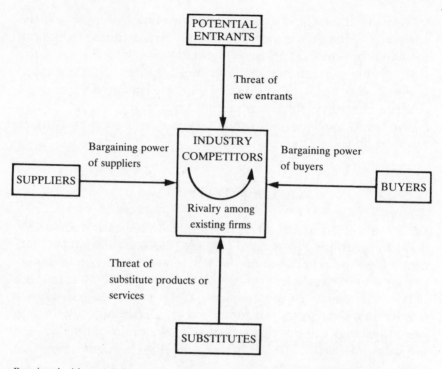

Reprinted with permission of The Free Press, a Division of Macmillan, Inc. from *Competitive Advantage: Creating and Sustaining Superior Performance* by Michael E. Porter. Copyright © 1985 by Michael E. Porter.

Figure 3   The five competitive forces that determine industry profitability

structure. However, this is not to say that a company cannot change an industry structure and consequently its underlying profitability. This happens all the time, as competitors change the way they compete with each other. None the less, a company has to understand its industry if it is to achieve such a fundamental shift. If we dissect the five forces this will become clear.

● Firstly, the bargaining power of suppliers will determine the degree of leverage they have. This will in turn be affected by a variety of issues such as the structure of the supplier's industry, the availability of substitute products and the degree of concentration in the client industry. Thus, if there are a number of competing companies, who can only buy their raw materials from one supplier, the bargaining power of the supplier will be high.

- Secondly, a similar situation exists for buyers. Generally, if the buying industry tends to be more concentrated than that supplying it, the buyers will wield greater power than the suppliers.

- Thirdly, the threat of substitute products has a potentially limiting power on the prices that companies can charge for their products or services. For example, if the cost of switching to a substitute product is low and its performance is high, then this will place pressure on an industry's competitors.

- Fourthly, the threat of new entrants places pressures on margins because of the need to build barriers to entry. Consequently, investments may need to be made by companies, not because they represent an optimal investment decision, but simply because they keep out a powerful competitor. This can be seen when companies integrate vertically to gain control either over the supply of raw materials, or over the means of distribution.

- Finally, the previous four factors combine to determine the intensity of rivalry among existing firms. If rivalry is intense it tends to impinge on prices and/or the quality of service, which will affect industry profitability.

Each industry will be different because the relative power of the five forces will be different and the factors determining the power of the forces — the industry structure — will vary. Similarly, each company will inter-act with the five forces in a different way because of its own unique identity, which will in turn determine its position within an industry. The five forces model's value lies in its ability to focus strategic thinking on those aspects of competition that are critical to success. An example serves to illustrate this point. An industry analysis of national newspapers in the UK shows a market where the five forces are undergoing a radical transformation.

Bargaining power of suppliers

Suppliers to newspapers are essentially equipment and paper suppliers. The whole basis of the relationship with equipment suppliers has changed over the last five years as computer typesetting and on-screen page make-up have replaced hot metal and litho processes. Secondly, the need for paper supplies has also begun to change as the facsimile transmission of made-up pages to printing sites at low-cost locations has made contract printing an option.

Bargaining power of buyers

There are two types of buyers of newspapers. The first is the consumer. These buyers of newspapers are obviously less concentrated than the publishers of newspapers. However, the ease with which buyers can switch to alternative titles or to other forms of communication is a price limitation. The second type of buyers are the advertisers and their agencies. In an attempt to increase their buying power, advertisers are increasingly centralizing their media buying capabilities in one media buying company or agency. The agencies themselves are also enhancing their relative weight by joint ventures in media buying, and, in the case of Saatchi and Saatchi, placing the media buying for their whole group of companies into one centralized unit known as Zenith. Thus, the overall bargaining power of advertisers is increasing.

Threat of substitutes

The threat of substitutes is high and is a major constraint on profitability. Consumer buyers can cease to purchase newspapers altogether or they can reduce their frequency of purchase. They can buy magazines, listen to the radio or watch television for up-to-date news, sport, current affairs and consumer interests. Advertising buyers can also switch into other media if a newspaper is found not to be cost-effective.

Threat of entrants

In the past the need to invest heavily in plant and labour was a deterrent to entry. The onset of new technology has taken away that deterrent, and it will in future be easier for new titles to appear and be profitable at lower circulation levels.

Intensity of competition

In recent years the UK has seen the successful launch of several national titles — *The Independent*, *Today* and the *Sport*. However, despite these new titles, readership continued to decline throughout the 1980s. Papers are having to compete more intensely with each other and with other forms of communication.

Thus, the key trends in the newspaper industry are the increasing threat of substitution by other forms of media and the reduction of entry barriers caused by the introduction of new technology. The ease with which the market can now be entered means that existing publishers will have to create defensible positions for themselves and reduce their operating overheads to a minimum in anticipation of increasing fragmentation and lower readership levels.

We can see from the analysis of this particular industry that there are a number of key issues to help determine how an organization should position itself for competitive success. To these issues the relevant macro-economic issues that apply at any given time have to be added. Thus, we should take account of the changing age profile of the population, levels of affluence, and the impact of European integration.

A picture of an industry will thus emerge, which will affect in a fundamental sense the corporate planning of newspapers. A successful strategy will take note of industry evolution and will address the requirements dictated by market forces. The strategy will also need to develop a coherent position for a given publication which not only takes account of the industry structure, but also the core strengths and weaknesses of the organization. The communication of that positioning to all the relevant audiences, through design and editorial style among other things, will help determine the success of the strategy.

Positioning

Having understood the key industry dynamics, the next task is to look at how an organization and its competitors are responding to

COMPETITIVE ADVANTAGE

		Lower Cost	Differentiation
COMPETITIVE SCOPE	Broad Target	1 Cost Leadership	2 Differentiation
	Narrow Target	3A Cost Focus	3B Differentiation Focus

Reprinted with permission of The Free Press, a Division of Macmillan, Inc. from *Competitive Advantage: Creating and Sustaining Superior Performance* by Michael E. Porter. Copyright © 1985 by Michael E. Porter.

Figure 4   Three generic strategies

the challenges created by industry evolution. At the end of this analytical phase we should be able to determine how organizations are positioned in relation to those key dynamics. This positioning will act as the guide for all communications both internally and externally. Again we can use a model developed by Michael Porter. He argues that although a company can have a variety of strengths and weaknesses, the basic means of gaining competitive advantage is through either cost advantage or differentiation. These in turn are derived from a company's ability to cope with the five competitive forces better than its rivals. If the two basic types of competitive advantage are combined with the scope of activities of a company, we arrive at a model that comprises three generic strategy options: cost leadership; differentiation; and focus, with a sub-division of the latter into cost and differentiation (Figure 4). Porter's view is that a company must make choices within this framework; that being stuck in the middle is the route to failure.

However, this does not preclude a company that has a generic strategy of differentiation from doing everything in its power to reduce costs, as long as it does not undermine the basis of its differentiation. To take an extreme example, Rolls Royce are clearly a company with a differentiation focus strategy. Their cars are very high quality products aimed at a very precise and wealthy niche that demands certain standards of their driving experience. To sustain the company's position the product offered has to be highly engineered which tends to mitigate against low costs. However, everything is done to reduce production costs without reducing product quality.

The need to be single minded

The rationale behind the need to choose a strategy is that a company will find it difficult to be both a cost leader and differentiated because each strategy requires total commitment and relevant structures to be successful. These tend to be mutually exclusive. One way round this is to develop or acquire subsidiary organizations that can focus on a particular market sector. Thus, Ford can be broadly based, while their subsidiary Jaguar can be focused.

It is also possible to change the generic strategy if this is found to be unsustainable. There are a number of examples of companies who have done this. In the US, Continental Bank had to be rescued by the Federal Deposit Insurance Corporation (FDIC), because the bank, like others in the US and the UK (Midland is the best British example), got into trouble because they believed their strongest position was derived from a broadly based service. Both Continental and Midland had to review their strategy in the wake of losses and then rebuild their operations with a more focused operation based on core strengths. Now Continental specializes in corporate banking, having eschewed the retail side of the business. Meanwhile, Midland has sold off Crocker, Clydesdale and Northern Banks and is focused on UK banking and wholesale.

Industry evolution and strategy shifts

We can also find examples of industry evolution within manufacturing which have caused companies to shift their strategies. The US car manufacturing industry has a history of continued evolution. Originally when Henry Ford developed his model T, he gained the advantage of being the lowest cost producer by achieving economies of scale through process innovation. Other car manufacturers then caught up with the assembly line method of production and the battleground shifted to broadly based differentiation built on marketing strengths. In the 1980s, the onslaught of Japanese manufacturers has brought a renewed focus on costs. Of the big three US producers, General Motors and Ford still have a differentiation strategy, although they have looked to reduce costs wherever possible to maintain competitiveness. Chrysler, on the other hand, has specifically set out to become the lowest cost producer among the US manufacturers. This is not to deny their attempts to improve quality, but their generic strategy is focused on cost.

Moving towards a market-oriented positioning

Similarly, the British float glass manufactuer, Pilkington plc, traditionally derived its advantage from the economies of scale achieved in the production process by having a patent on float glass technology. It was thus a low cost producer, much like ICI in its pre-added value and 'World Class' days. However, the main source of advantage now is the combination of technology management allied to marketing. The company has successfully acquired new businesses in allied glass areas and has derived a high income stream from the judicious sale of licence arrangements for the float glass technology. As with much of British business in recent years, Pilkington has moved away from a production to a customer focus — from commodity to added value products and from low cost to differentiation.

Whatever strategy a company chooses it has to be:

- representative of the company's strengths;

- relevant to the consumers of a company's products;

- communicated to all relevant audiences;
- sustainable against competitive threats over time.

Just as it has to make choices about how to position its brands, so a company has to make a choice about its overall position in relation to its competitors. First of all this should be defined in broad terms, based on differentiation or cost leadership. Then the strategy should be defined in more precise terms, so that the organization knows precisely how it is going to be differentiated, or which target markets it is going to focus in on. Once this has been agreed, all the company's activities have to work cohesively and single-mindedly towards achieving competitive advantage. Getting the activities to work together goes beyond corporate strategy and into the management of everything the organization does. It centres on the long-term management of the corporate identity itself.

Summary

1. Identity and strategy are closely inter-related. The strategy will be influenced by the identity, while the identity will be affected by the nature of the strategy.

2. To determine the best strategy requires an understanding of the forces that drive competition within an industry.

3. Having determined the industry structure, we need to analyse a company's positioning strategy. A company that has a clear generic strategy, according to Porter, is likely to perform well. A company that does not pursue a clear strategy will tend to be stuck in the middle and thus perform poorly.

4. Once a generic strategy has been adopted the key requirement is that a company pursues it single-mindedly in everything it does. Otherwise, the strategy will be compromised.

References

[1] Philip Kotler, *Marketing Management: analysis, planning and control*, 5th edn (Prentice Hall, 1984) p 34
[2] Brian Dumaine, 'Cover Story on P&G', *Fortune International* (6 November 1989).

4

THE CORPORATE IDENTITY

Although a strategy may guide the direction of an organization, it will only be effective if the organization itself is managed effectively to support that direction. The implication of this is that all the elements of an organization which collectively form the identity need to support and enhance the competitive advantage that the strategy is seeking to achieve. On this premise, this chapter will look at the component parts of a corporate identity and also examine how some specific organizations successfully manage their identities.

Uncovering the Corporate Identity

Although we can quite quickly form an image of an organization, establishing its identity is a far more difficult task. To uncover the real identity we need to break the organization down into its component parts, and look at the organization in two ways. First, we need to look at the components of the identity, such as the organizational history, the nature of ownership and the shared values. Secondly, we need to look at how these factors work within the various business units and the functional departments of the organization. This will then give us a picture of the organizational identity — the sum of the parts — as well as a picture of the business unit identities.

To break the organization down in this fashion takes a concerted research programme involving a number of sources. These sources are looked at below.

Published sources

These can be extensive or extremely limited, depending on the relative newness/obscurity of the industry and the company. However, a good place to start is to collect the publications produced by a company, including the annual report and accounts and then conduct a database search on one of the many media monitoring databases. This should provide both information in its own right and also clues to further sources. These would include statistical data produced either by government bodies or by trade associations. For example, the Brewers' Society produces extensive and regular data about consumption patterns and related issues on the UK Brewing Industry.

Finally, most major industries have studies written on them either by research firms, who then sell the reports, or by securities companies who will produce both generalized and focused reports on specific aspects of an industry. This desk research phase should be conducted before the interview programme as it will give a basis of knowledge with which to conduct the interviews and also highlight any specific areas that look contentious and may need to be probed.

Interview programme

The first part of the interview programme is to determine a list of interviewees. Inevitably, the interview list will evolve as some issues become more important or more difficult to resolve than others, but as a starting point the interview programme should move from the general to the specific. The following groups of people should all be considered:

- management;
- employees from all departments;
- journalists;
- market analysts;
- trade associations;
- consultants;
- auditors;

- advertising agencies;

- government;

- international organizations;

- industry commentators/experts.

Having first determined who we are going to talk to, a loosely structured discussion guide needs to be developed. Rather than slavishly following a set of questions, the guide will steer the conversation with interviewees allowing the analyst to probe issues that are particularly important to the respondent, or that the analyst senses are relevant. Although any external analyst may bring their own cultural values and perceptions to an interview, their relative objectivity when compared to an internal inter-viewer should always enable the process to be more informative.

What emerges in most interview programmes is that if the shared set of values and sense of history are strong, such as in the case of IBM, the expressed views about the identity are likely to be similar. If the organization is relatively new, has a poor sense of shared values, or encourages individualism without control, such as within an academic institution, for example, the expressed views are likely to be dissimilar.

Direct experience

It may not always be practicable to experience an organization at first hand, but if it can be done it can yield evidence that would be hard to come by using any other means. For example, it is often extremely difficult to understand the degree of inter-manager conflict that is acceptable to an organization by listening to someone in the organization telling you about it. It is much better to sit in on a group meeting and see it for yourself. The experience of being told by senior management that their organ-ization is a picture of harmony, where everyone works to a common goal, is very familiar. In reality there is often not only conflict, but potentially damaging attitudes such as the deliberate sabotage of group objectives in favour of business unit or depart-mental objectives.

One example of a company where the projected attitude of harmony masked cultural conflict was Renault Truck Industries, the UK arm of Renault Vehicules Industriels. Renault had gained a foothold in the UK by acquiring Dodge Trucks from Peugeot, who had bought Dodge some years earlier from Chrysler. Renault were trying to present a picture of a unified organization, and had even been through a corporate identity programme in the early 1980s to create a greater sense of equality and unity. The reality was that although Renault had their senior managers in place in such areas as marketing, the engineering and production departments were still controlled by what was known internally as the 'Dodge Mafia', a group of senior managers who had been with the company through its various changes of management. The pervading attitude among these managers was 'We've seen it all before'. So as fast as Renault managers tried to move the company forwards, negative attitudes in key areas held it back. This fundamental barrier to progress would not have been recognized by simply talking to senior Renault managers. It had to be actually experienced.

The process of organizational analysis should use all these research methods to uncover the real corporate identity. However, the relative success of the process will depend to a large measure on the degree of support received from senior management and, more specifically, the Chief Executive. Without this endorsement, barriers can emerge which will effectively prevent accurate analysis. This can have severe consequences, because the initial research will be the basis for future assumptions and solutions. Get the early stages wrong and the whole programme may be strategically misplaced. Thus, any study of the organizational reality must be comprehensive. Although this may not require an in-depth study of all the following issues, they should certainly be considered as the organization is analysed.

Ownership

Ownership will affect the identity of the organization in two ways. First, the very nature of ownership tends to confer certain types of attributes. A small, privately owned company is likely to have a different type of identity to a government-owned monopoly, while an independent company will have a different psyche to a subsidiary of a multinational. Ownership is important because it helps to determine loyalties, degrees of independence, motivation, the saliency of unit objectives against group objectives, reporting relationships, and reward systems.

A company that is privately owned can be built around the vision of one person. That person's view of the world and of human relationships will determine the nature of the corporate identity. Thus, the personality of the owner/manager will be a key determinant in the type of corporate culture that emerges. It is often very difficult to disassociate a leader's personality from his/her organization. Richard Branson helps create an adventurous, youthful image for his company, Virgin, by the type of person he is. To most of the world Tiny Rowland *is* Lonrho. His buccaneering spirit exemplifies the way the organization is perceived to do business.

In contrast, a government-owned monopoly, such as British Coal, will tend to lack the power of a personality who is associated over a long period of time with the organization. It will also have a set of objectives determined not only by its own management, but also in part by government attitudes and, more specifically, the current British government's desire to privatize.

Secondly, a change in ownership is an oft-cited catalyst for identity programmes, and this is one of those factors that can change the corporate identity in a radical way. One set of beliefs may be completely replaced by another, or there may be a fusion of two sets of beliefs. If we take the example of a leveraged buyout we can see how a change of ownership can affect the objectives of an organization.

Beatrice, the US conglomerate, was purchased by a group of investors led by Kohlberg Kravis and Roberts (KKR) in 1986. Since the acquisition for \$8.2 billion, large tranches of the business have been disposed of. The buyout needed to make sure that the judicious disposal of the component parts of the company would help the investment group to realize a profit. Ownership by KKR has imposed a set of objectives concerned with maximizing the potential of assets so that profits can be sweated out of them, or so that they can be sold on. Thus, ownership in this instance promotes short-term interests and creates a resultant uncertainty. The culture has moved from a state of relative stability to a state of considerable flux.

Acquisitions and identities

In the case of a merger or acquisition, there are two potential results: one is a merging of identities, while the other is a subsuming of one identity. A good example of the former was the acquisition of Sperry Univac by Burroughs to form a new entity called Unisys. Both these companies had long histories, strong cultures and a large number of long serving employees. Sperry Univac was very homogeneous and had a tradition of slow, steady change. Burroughs, in its more recent history, was less homogeneous and had begun to thrive on change. Although Burroughs was the acquirer, the process was presented as a merger. This was because the new company was determined to merge the identities, rather than allow one company to dominate the other. For this reason the company decided to formulate a new name to demonstrate that the best of both identities had been brought together to form a new organization. As Jeanette Lerman of Unisys says: 'The internal audience had to be convinced about the legitimacy of ideas. There were to be no victors or vanquished.'

Compare this thinking with the other approach to acquisitions where one party emerges as the definitive senior partner. Sometimes, in an attempt to preserve morale and motivation, companies try to get round the victor/vanquished syndrome by retaining the name of the acquired company on equal status for a while before relegating it to a brand or divisional name, and then allowing it to disappear altogether. As Gene Grossman, of identity consultants Anspach Grossman Portugal, says: 'Through acquisition company names and their goodwill can disappear completely or become brands rather than corporations, thus lowering their profile.'

This works if the holding company tries to integrate the two cultures and if sufficient cooling-off time is allowed. However, there have been notable instances where the identities of the two partners have been so dissimilar that the change of ownership has led to a rapid disappearance of one identity.

Such was the fate of the highly successful UK advertising agency, Reeves Robertshaw, which was acquired by Doyle Dane Bernbach (DDB), one of the foremost names in advertising. Reeves Robertshaw was an aggressive go-getting agency and quite unlike the more relaxed and creatively sophisticated DDB, which over the decades had produced highly distinctive and creative campaigns, most notably for Volkswagen. Twelve months after the acquisition, Reeves Robertshaw's client base had all but disappeared, as had all the senior personnel. DDB has not been the only company to suffer this fate, but in a service business like advertising, where you are acquiring people and clients, the value of an acquisition is negated if both of those disappear rapidly.

Nationality and identities

One further impact of ownership is the nationality of the owners. For example, Japanese owners have a different set of cultural and business values to US owners, and they bring those values to an organizational setting. These differences can be appreciated by looking at time horizons. US companies have extremely short time horizons because of the requirement to publish financial results on a quarterly basis. The UK is not much better with its six-monthly time horizon. Public companies in both these countries tend to be under considerable pressure to turn in good performances all the time. This tends to mitigate against taking a long-term view of a problem. Steven Gilliatt, of identity consultants Lippincott & Margulies, endorses this:

> The US is a little bit overboard in terms of stock reporting requirements, because most companies are run on a quarterly basis here, and that doesn't allow the typical CEO to establish the long term visions. If you want to take a loss for the next two quarters, because you're building for the future, you find that shareholders don't really understand that.

The Japanese company, on the other hand, supported by loyal institutional investors and an understanding government, in the form of the Ministry of International Trade and Industry (MITI), is able and willing to take a longer term perspective of a problem. This moves the identity away from a concern with short-term performance indicators to an interest in building market share and long-term well-being.

As will now be obvious, it is not the *fact* of ownership that is important, but the *values* conferred by it. Ownership traits are relevant because of the priorities they set. Sometimes the priority is the pursuit of growth objectives, such as Unisys setting out to establish critical mass and to challenge IBM more effectively.

Sometimes it is out of necessity, such as the loss-making International Harvester brand being sold by its owners, to ensure corporate survival. Whichever scenario is appropriate, the analyst must be aware of the nature of corporate ownership and the resultant set of priorities which it implies.

Corporate and Product Performance

If, at a subsequent stage in the analytical process, we are going to investigate and judge an organization's communications and the perceptions that are created, we need to confirm at an early stage the quality of the product and corporate performance. For example, we cannot say that a company is undervalued until we have established what the value should be. If undervaluation exists we need to know what has caused the undervaluation. Benchmarks need to be established for all a company's products and for the organization itself.

At the corporate level, one of the most useful tools is the PAR report of the PIMS (profit impact of market strategies) database,[1] which is administered by the Strategic Planning Institute (SPI), and compares the actual profitability (Return on Investment) of an organization to its PAR value. The PAR value is the anticipated return on investment. This is arrived at by utilizing the information on a database which allows the characteristics of the company under analysis to be matched against companies with similar characteristics. The PAR value is determined by the scores of the business against key performance indicators such as market share and relative spending on research and design (Figure 5). Given a company's strategic profile, we can determine what the return on investment should be, and then match this against the actual return on investment. Bernard Reimann, in his book *Managing for Value*, explains the purpose of PIMS thus:

> The basic intent of the PIMS program is to identify a set of underlying principles of successful business strategy or 'laws of the marketplace', based on extensive empirical research. A great many statistical analyses have been made over the years, as the PIMS data bank has grown from a few hundred to nearly 3000 businesses. Originally most of the work was done

The Corporate Image

EXCERPT FROM A PIMS ROI REPORT
IMPACTS OF ROI-INFLUENCING FACTORS:
A DIAGNOSIS OF STRATEGIC STRENGTHS
AND WEAKNESSES

SPI
I
M
S

Bus. XXXX
20-Mar-87

	PIMS MEAN	THIS BUSINESS	IMPACT	–SENSITIVITY– A DATA CHANGE OF	ALTERS IMPACT BY
COMPETITIVE POSITION			**-0.9**		
Market Share Index			-0.6		1.8
Market Share	23.4	23.0		4.0	
Relative Market Share	62.1	34.7	10.0		
Relative Product Quality	25.8	20.0	-0.8	6.0	0.8
Relative Price	103.7	103.5	0.0	1.0	-0.2
Relative Direct Cost	101.8	100.0	0.8	1.0	-0.4
Patents re Process or Products	0.4	2.0	-0.4	0.1	0.0
Rel. Range of Customer Size		same	0.1		
STAGE OF LIFE CYCLE			**0.4**		
Real Market Growth, Long Run	4.2	-3.1	-0.3	2.0	-0.4
Unionization (%)	43.0	75.0	-1.9	7.0	-0.7
New Products (% of Sales)	10.3	11.0	1.9	3.0	-0.6
Research & Development/ Sales	2.2	5.5	0.8	0.5	0.2
Selling-Price Growth Rate	7.6	7.1	-0.1	1.0	0.3
MARKETING ENVIRONMENT			**1.6**		
Marketing/Sales	9.3	2.3	1.2	1.0	0.0
Purchase Amount-Immed. Cust.	$10,000	-$1MM	-0.8		
% of all End User's Purchases		>25%	1.4		
No. Customers = 50% of Sales	337.2	265.6	-1.3	100.0	-0.5
Products Produced to Order		No	0.2		
Industry Concentration	57.5	80.0	0.9	5.0	0.2
CAPITAL & PRODUCTION STRUCTURE			**-3.1**		
Investment Intensity Index			-0.7		-1.5
Investment/Sales	52.8	49.6		5.0	
Investment/Value Added	96.0	89.3		8.0	
Production Effectiveness	100.0	88.3	-2.1	6.0	0.9
Capacity Utilization	75.6	91.3	2.6	3.0	0.4
G.B.V. of P&E/Investment	89.1	130.1	-1.4	10.0	-0.2
Vertical Integration	56.0	55.5	0.0	3.0	0.2
Investment/Employee ($1973)	29.8	25.0	0.0	6.0	-0.9

Relative Employee Compensation	100.7	87.5	1.9	1.0	−0.2
Shared Production Facilities		<10%	−0.5		
Accounting Convention		FIFO	−0.1		
Receivables/Investment	32.7	14.1	−2.2	4.0	0.4
Raw Matls. & W-in-P/Val. Added	21.5	31.1	−0.6	3.0	−0.2

SUMMARY: **IMPACT (in percentage points):**

COMPETITIVE POSITION	−0.9
STAGE OF LIFE CYCLE	0.4
MARKETING ENVIRONMENT	1.6
CAPITAL & PRODUCTION STRUCTURE	−3.1
SUM OF IMPACTS	−2.0
+ AVG. RETURN ON INVESTMENT	22.1%
'PAR' RETURN ON INVESTMENT	20.1%

Source: PIMS Europe Ltd. Reprinted by permission

Figure 5   Excerpt from a PIMS ROI Report

by SPI and its associates, but more recently the data has been made available to the academic community.[2]

However, even without using the PAR report, we can use the annual report and accounts and stockbroker's evaluations to learn about revenues, the level of profits, the cost of sales, costs of administration, and numerous other indicators. When we then look at the trend data to check how the company has been doing over time, both in terms of year-on-year growth, and by using comparative ratio reports in relation to the competition, we can form a fairly accurate idea of the corporate position.

The next important phase is to assess the performance of a company's products. Products can affect the identity in three respects.

● Firstly, the quality of product can affect the perceived value of the company. This is especially noticeable when a product can have a significant impact on future profits, such as in pharmaceuticals. ICI knows this to its cost: 'Reports that its diabetics drug Statil had produced disappointing evidence in clinical trials and the heart drug Corwin could make severe heart problems worse sent the share price plummeting ahead of results.'[3]

- Secondly, the type of product sold can influence the identity. A company that has an historically strong identity as a manufacturer of a product will sometimes move away from that base into a service industry or allied product areas. As a consequence, the identity of the company will evolve because of the product portfolio. For example, Bausch & Lomb had a 130-year history as a manufacturer in hard optics. However, with acquisitions, the product portfolio has changed so that the company now has become essentially a service-oriented health-care company. The question is, have the company's key audiences kept up with the changing corporate profile? We can judge this when we come to look at the perceptions of a company, and determine whether there is any difference between the product reality and those perceptions. We can only do this if we have established benchmarks from which to make a judgement.

- Thirdly, for some audiences, the product *is* the company. Often consumers will have no other contact with a company other than through advertising and the purchase of its products. For example, the purchasers of a Volvo car would see Volvo as a company in terms of the performance of its car and its after-sales service. If the car is well thought out this would suggest to the consumer that the company pays attention to detail. Similarly, the image a consumer has of a Ferrari as a superbly engineered product would carry over to the perception of the company itself. Brand and corporate image become largely indivisible.

When measuring product performance, we need to look at key indicators such as market share and profitability. We need to have a view as to which products are successful now and which are likely to be successful in the future. And we need to look at how the product structure relates to the corporate structure.

Structure

A key component of a corporate identity is the corporate structure. However, in reality there are two structures. There is the organizational structure with its lines of communication and reporting responsibilities. Then there is the visual structure, which concerns itself with the branding of products, business units and the corporate umbrella and how they are presented to an organization's audiences. The organizational structure will be dealt with here: the visual structure will be dealt with in Chapter 8.

The fundamental concern with the organizational structure is the degree of centralization and decentralization. A subsidiary in a highly decentralized structure is likely to have an identity of its own. For example, Glaxo Holdings, the British pharmaceutical company, operates a highly decentralized organization. Overall strategy is determined at group headquarters, but it is then up to each individual country to take on the strategy in its local market. As Geoffrey Potter, Director of Corporate Communications for Glaxo, says: 'The structure stems from a deep seated belief that you can't run businesses in local markets from the centre ... those markets are the best judge as to how to position each drug in the market.'

The only unifying forces within Glaxo are the nature of the pharmaceuticals business, where direct relationships between the individual salesman and the physician are the norm, and the fact that the same product portfolio is sold throughout the world. Any communication between countries tends to be informal and not imposed from the centre. This corporate structure creates companies in each country with their own distinctive identities. The pull towards the centre is built primarily around financial accountability. This is not to suggest that the company fails to communicate its broad strategy to the operating companies, but it does not seek to impose uniformity or a universal identity. As a demonstration of this there is no central control over the use of logos in any markets.

In direct contrast to this type of highly decentralized structure, there are companies who operate highly centralized structures, which deny local autonomy and control all key functions at the centre. The identity in this instance (if the company is good at communicating its corporate value system) will be strongly similar in both the parent and the subsidiary. However, the reality for most companies is that they are a mixture of decentralized and centralized operations and, consequently, subsidiaries will be a mixture of their own individual identities, while owing something to their parentage. Michael Porter make this point in his discussion of inter-relationships between business units:

Inter-relationships are also facilitated if the corporate identity is displayed prominently in each business unit on logos, signs and stationery. This does not imply the abandonment of valuable business unit trade names. Instead it suggests that a firm should develop both its corporate identity as well as those of its business units, within the firm and outside.[4]

Leaders, Employees and Shared Values

Every organization with a history has a set of values that determine and direct its thinking. Those values will generally be taken for granted, and will not be questioned by the members of an organization, provided they enable those individuals to deal with both internal and external events successfully. When an organization confronts failure, it may seek security in its value system, or the value system may be confronted. Which route is chosen depends on how strongly individuals are imbued with the same values. They will tend to be stronger when there is a stable employment pattern with a large number of long-serving employees. Shared values will only become shared by sharing experiences of success and failure over a period of time. Until this happens truth will be individual rather than corporate.

IBM

The degree of homogeneity in an organization will be determined by how deeply the values are rooted. In an organization such as IBM, they are deep. Values are shared right across the organizational structure. This is because Thomas J Watson worked hard to instil his own view of the world, and IBM's role within it, to all his employees. The three core beliefs that he and his sons bequeathed the company are still very much in evidence:

● First and most important is 'respect for the individual'. This was seen by Tom Watson Jr as the most important factor in IBM's success: 'I believe the real difference between success and failure in a corporation can very often be traced to the question of how well the organization brings out the great energies and talents of its people. I believe that if an organization is to meet the challenges of a changing world it must be prepared to change everything about itself except its basic beliefs.'[5]

- Second is full employment. Once an employee joins IBM, they are there for life if they want to be.

- Third is single status, which implies a sense of equality for all employees, whatever their background and position.

These beliefs could, however, amount to nothing if they were not shared by a majority of the staff. Simply producing a leaflet about core values or beliefs will not ensure ownership of a common idea. Beliefs have to be seen in action. Leaders have to convey their beliefs in their decisions and their pronouncements.

Federal Express

Federal Express is another company that impresses with its sense of shared values. Frederick W Smith of Federal Express says: 'People respond to what they see and hear, not what you write down.'[6]

The two things that stand out about Federal Express are not so dissimilar from IBM. One is its customer orientation. The other is its seemingly genuine concern for its employees. These two views interlink. The values that senior management convey to staff are trust and pride. Trust in the individual and pride in the quality of work.

This feeling is then carried on by staff in their dealings with customers. How then are these values communicated? How do they come to be shared? The first point to note is that the values are highly acceptable. A value system that encouraged mistrust and an 'us-and-them' attitude would be less appealing, although one could argue that it is still endemic in much of British industry. Secondly, a series of mechanisms are in place that help engender corporate-wide beliefs. These include the actions of leaders, the views they disseminate, the response to problems, and the ways and means of communication. Although one may view with some scepticism the pronouncements to be found in the annual report and accounts and any other official publications of an organization, the Federal Express Annual Report confirms what can be observed elsewhere in the organization.

The very first page of the report features a message about the company's commitment to Equal Employment Opportunities. Not only does this give an official message, but it also adds: 'We are strongly bound to this commitment because adherence to Equal Employment Opportunity principles is the only acceptable American way of life. We adhere to those principles not just because they're the law, but because it's the right thing to do.'

Elsewhere in the report, we find pictures of the employees. It has always been a bugbear of Tom Peters, the forthright co-author of *In Search of Excellence*, that whereas management pictures in annual reports always have name and title captions, the employees are always nameless. His argument is that this shows a disregard for the importance and individuality of the work-force. The Federal Express report provides both the names and the positions of the employees featured, and it endorses its equal opportunities message by featuring people from a variety of ethnic origins.

Then, when we move into the core of the report, we find a more overt statement about the company's people principles.

> The best technology in the world is useless, of course, unless it is in the hands of a well-trained and highly motivated workforce. Maintaining high levels of job satisfaction has always been of paramount concern at Federal Express, a company whose personnel policies have generally been considered among the most progessive and innovative in America. Because of employees' consistent efforts, the company's reputation for courteous and efficient customer service remains second to none.

The reality is that all the pronouncements of the annual report could be just cosmetic. After all, one of the core audiences for the report are the employees themselves. However, I would suggest that the concern is genuine. The media statements of the two key personnel, Frederick W Smith (Chairman, President and CEO) and James L Barksdale (Executive Vice President and Chief Operating Officer) consistently convey a belief in the work-force.

In turn, employees seem to take great pride in their job, will quote very readily what their company stands for and put into practice the principles of service they espouse. They have high degrees of autonomy and involvement. For example, it was the couriers, not a design department, that designed the company uniform. Similarly, of all the annual report and accounts I have requested from companies, Federal Express was the only one who had an executive of the company deliver it to my office.

Finally, almost as an aside, but one which demonstrates corporate pride, wherever one goes in the world Federal Express vehicles are spotlessly clean.

The strength of Federal Express's shared values is such that a strongly cohesive and consistent identity is created. The beliefs of the leaders have been effectively communicated, employees represent those beliefs in their actions and reactions to events, and the reward systems are geared to ensuring involvement. This gives the company the best of both worlds — a ubiquitous image and high levels of employee responsibility and motivation.

However, before we conclude that this corporate single-mindedness is a universally good thing, we should note two points. Firstly, creating a strong sense of shared values can result in blindness to opportunities and threats, unless questioning is one of the values promoted. Charles Handy, in his book *Understanding Organisations*, quotes I L Janis's *Victims of Group Think* (1972) which demonstrates the danger:

> 'How could we have been so stupid?' asked President John F Kennedy, after he and a group of close advisers had blundered into the Bay of Pigs invasion.
>
> Stupidity was certainly not the explanation. The group who made the decision was one of the greatest collections of intellectual talent in the history of American Government. Irving Janis describes the blunder as a result of 'group think'.
>
> 'Group think' occurs when too high a price is placed on the harmony and morale of the group, so that loyalty to the group's previous policies, or to the group consensus, overrides the conscience of each member.[7]

Secondly, some companies derive their competitive advantage from decentralized structures, so autonomous business units may well have strong identities of their own. In this instance, therefore, the single-mindedness may reside more within the business unit structure, rather than within the corporate whole.

Understanding corporate values is the key to understanding the nature of an identity. The values will help determine key attributes of the organization. The reward systems will be decided by the corporate attitude to motivation. The emphasis placed on training and career development will be based on an idea of the importance of individuals. The decision-making processes will be guided by the value placed on corporate harmony and the degree of autonomy. All these values can be seen in action in a company.

Further, as the Federal Express example demonstrated, clues as to the values come from the official publications of an organization, the attitudes and beliefs of leaders, the actions of individuals and the small organizational details of daily life, such as clean trucks.

Summary

1. To understand an identity, the organization needs to be broken down into its component parts. The process of analysis then involves desk research, interviews and direct experience.

2. The identity is determined by a number of factors which include the nature of ownership, corporate and product performance, the corporate structure, the beliefs of leaders, and the sharing of values.

3. One of the most frequent catalysts of corporate identity programmes is a change in ownership. However, even without change, the type of ownership tends to confer certain types of identity. The nationality of the owners, the size of the organization, and the dominance by individuals will all affect the identity.

4. So that we can judge at a later stage in the analysis whether the perceptions of the company and its products are better or worse than the reality, performance indicators need to be established.

5. There is a difference between the organizational and the visual structure. The organizational structure is important to a

corporate identity to the extent that it will determine the relationship of parent company values to those of business units.

6. What really determines the strength of the organizational identity is the extent to which values are commonly held in an organization. In companies like Federal Express and IBM they appear to be very strong. This is because the values are clearly defined, and supported and endorsed not only by words, but also, more importantly, by actions and leadership.

References

[1] Bernard C Reimann, *Managing For Value. A guide to value-based strategic management* (The Planning Forum, 1987)
[2] *ibid*, p 216
[3] *The Guardian* (18 July 1989) p 14
[4] Michael Porter, *Competitive Advantage* (The Free Press, 1985) p 408
[5] David Mercer, *IBM: How the World's Most Successful Corporation is Managed* (Kogan Page, 1987), p 206 and quoting from *Employment with IBM* (1962)
[6] Frederick W Smith, 'The Big Company' on Channel 4
[7] From Charles Handy, *Understanding Organisations*, 3rd edn (Penguin Books, 1985)

5

THE COMMUNICATIONS
AUDIT

Having determined the nature of the corporate identity, the next phase in the analytical process is to determine how effectively the identity and the corporate strategy is communicated. This process is known as a visual or communications audit and is comprised of two elements. The first is the collation, monitoring and assessment of all forms of internal and external communication. This process is normally conducted by an identity consultant, who is seeking to determine the logic and consistency of communication. The second is a research-based phase among the various audiences of a company to determine the impact of all overt and non-overt communications on their perception of the company.

Inevitably these two aspects are linked. If, for example, in conducting the initial communications audit, it is discovered that employees have no means of communicating across an organizational structure, then it will not be surprising to discover when those employees are interviewed, a limited understanding or a confused image of how other divisions in the organization operate.

Although, in reality, the process of communications audit and audience perceptions would normally be conducted simultaneously, for our purposes they will be better broken down into two chapters. Chapter 5 will focus on the practical problems of assessment, while Chapter 6 will concentrate on the perceptions created.

Undertaking an Audit

External printed communications

The communications audit begins with the collection of all forms of printed and visual communication, whether it be the annual report and accounts, product brochures, letterheads, corporate advertisements or quotations from the chief executive. The amount of printed material can be enormous and is often instructive in its scale. Whereas in smaller and medium-sized companies the commissioning of design work and print buying will often be centralized, in large, diversified organizations, print and design often emanates from several different sources. Each department or subsidary will have its own budget, and will commission its own work. As more and more companies decentralize their operations there is a danger that the communication process can get out of control. A company the size of AT&T can literally have hundreds of advertising, design and PR agencies.

As well as collecting the communications of the company under consideration, the key communications of competitors should also be obtained. This will provide a basis for comparing the quality and tenor of the client's communications.

Once everything has been collated there are many ways of assessing the information. The important point to remember is that what we are looking to determine is whether the communication accurately reflects the identity of the organization and its strategic direction. We are looking for the points of consistency and, more importantly, the points of inconsistency. The question that should be asked as we look at leaflets and advertisements is 'Is a clear and accurate picture of this organization emerging from its communications?' For example, if a company has adopted a differentiation focus strategy built around quality of service, we need to determine whether the communications endorse or confuse that positioning. This is a relatively easy task with a small organization, but a large organization demands an holistic approach.

One very good means of doing this is to put everything in one room, and examine the key messages that come across from all a company's communications. When Lippincott & Margulies undertook an identity management project for AT&T's Consumer

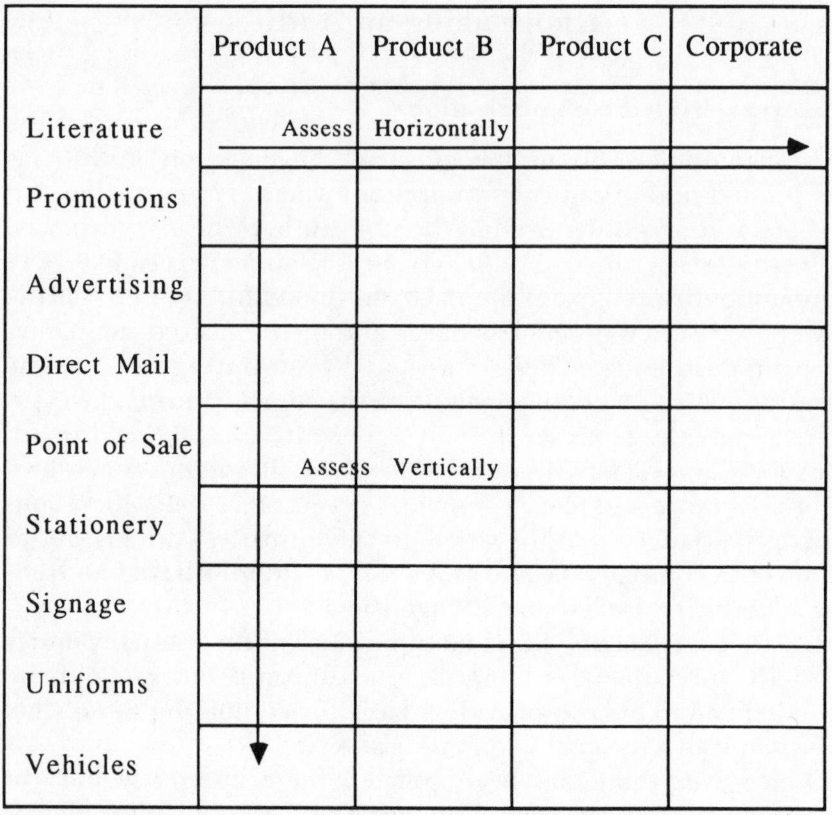

	Product A	Product B	Product C	Corporate
Literature	Assess	Horizontally		➔
Promotions				
Advertising				
Direct Mail				
Point of Sale	Assess	Vertically		
Stationery				
Signage				
Uniforms				
Vehicles	▼			

Figure 6   A communications matrix

Communications Services group, the one room became six rooms with 10 000 ft^2 of space full of material.

Once the information is in one place it needs to be grouped so it can be analysed rationally. This grouping should be done in two ways (Figure 6).

● Firstly, it should be grouped vertically product by product. Thus, if a potential customer were to receive all the communications relating to one product, what would the sum of those messages be? Do the advertising, packaging, sales brochures, direct mail and in-store promotions all convey a consistent message?

● Secondly, the grouping should be completed horizontally. We are looking here to assess how the communications for all a company's products work by media type. If it is important that there is a consistent message in all product advertising, does that come through? If a consumer receives a mail shot from three different product divisions of the same company, it will be potentially very confusing if they each present a different picture of the organization.

Once the communications matrix has been assessed in these two forms, the full impact of all vertical and horizontal communications needs to be analysed.

To give an example, the Royal Opera House in Covent Garden is the 'holding company' of three performing companies: the Royal Opera; the Royal Ballet; and the Birmingham Royal Ballet. To assess the communications of the total organization, we need first to place ourselves in the position of someone who is only interested in the Royal Opera and look at the level of vertical consistency. Then we need to place ourselves in the position of someone who is interested in both ballet and opera, and assess the continuity horizontally across the various communication mechanisms.

Finally, if we imagine ourselves in the position of a member of the government or the Arts Council (who provide the Royal Opera House with a grant), we need to know how the sum of the communications emanating from the Royal Opera House, including the more corporate forms such as the annual report and accounts, add up.

What we are searching for in the analytical matrix is the organizational logic, as it is presented to the company's audiences. Thus, we are looking to establish:

- Whether there is logic in the company's naming policies. Do three divisions of a company use one consistent juxtaposition of names, while a fourth uses another? Do the names accurately reflect the activities of each division?

- Whether there is logic in graphic presentation. Do divisions look like part of the same company? Are they conveying a consistent identity and strategic direction?

- Whether the language used is appropriate. Is the tone correct? Is it easy to understand?

Wally Olins, of the design consultancy Wolff Olins, once described corporate identity as 'the visualization of strategy'. If we did not know the corporate strategy for an organization, the final acid test of the communications audit would be to see if the strategy comes through accurately from the assembled information.

Internal communications

This first phase has concentrated on printed material, mainly that aimed at external audiences. Two additional audits should also be conducted. The first of these is the assessment of internal communications. At the more obvious level, this will include employee publications, both those which are officially supported and those which are not. The official publications, such as company newspapers and magazines, are most often run by PR or press departments. In addition to reporting on company events, they will be used as a means of disseminating management information and strategies. The editorial quality of in-house publications varies enormously from the banal and mundane to the occasionally stimulating. The alternative employee newspaper that exists in some companies however, is often more instructive than the official staff publication. This will sometimes contain the real picture of employee attitudes.

The other type of internal communication ranges from the everyday putting of information on noticeboards and sending of memos, to the more irregular public announcements, annual conferences and seminars. Again all these activities are primarily important for the way they communicate strategy and enhance the identity of the organization. Their effectiveness in doing so can only be judged when we come to look at the perceptions created. Of course, the difficulty in all this is measuring the scale of non-communication. If the strategy is singularly failing to get through to employees, it may be because the management are simply not fulfilling their duty to communicate to employees, or it may be that the organizational culture has traditionally placed a low priority on internal communications.

Less obvious means of Communication

The second audit involves the less obvious methods of communication. These include all the details of daily business life from the way the telephone is answered, to the way sales people act, to the way people dress. All these details are important because they reflect the corporate value system. The fact that everyone at McDonald's smiles suggests that McDonald's takes care of its staff and is a good place to work. When Federal Express's vehicles are all spotlessly clean, it suggests care and attention to detail.

Office or retail environments are also an important part of the communication process. For example, when Prudential embarked upon a corporate identity programme, they also decided to redesign their antiquated and overly imposing head office in London. In keeping with their overall corporate objective of maintaining the secure and solid image of the company, while introducing a lighter, more modern touch, the exterior of the building was retained, but the interior has been redeveloped to make it more consumer friendly. Architecture and interior design is as much an expression of the corporate identity as anything else. As Maxwell Hutchinson, President of the Royal Institute of British Architects notes:

> Buildings have always been part of the corporate image. I mean look at the great Victorian railway builders. They built St Pancras Station, this great work of architectural fiction, to reinforce their image of themselves. The Great Eastern Railway built Liverpool Street for the same reason. The Daily Telegraph has built this building [in London's Docklands] as a personification and as a symbol of its change, and I believe it has helped to reinforce that change.[1]

Similarly, in a retail operation, the nature and quality of product presentation, the logic of placing one product group next to another and the store's ambience will all communicate a certain message. In this situation, the ground rules still apply. We are looking at the store to determine the logic of its communications and to determine whether they accurately reflect strategy.

Whatever the nature of an organization's communications, we need to form a complete picture. At this stage we are only making a subjective judgement about the saliency of the messages being sent out. Areas of concern can be pinpointed, inconsistencies can be seen and control systems determined. As to whether the company is achieving true economies of communication, or whether the corporate structure is accurately presented, can only be determined by asking the relevant audiences what they take out of an organization's communications.

The perceptions of the company and the consequent definition of the corporate image will be addressed in Chapter 6. For the moment we should note that the communications audit is not only concerned with the design function, but also the quality and relevance of communication in all its forms.

Summary

1. The communications audit is the process by which the analyst assesses whether or not the organization is communicating its identity and strategy effectively.

2. It comprises the collation, monitoring and assessment of all forms of printed and visual communication.

3. In addition to the visual audit, the consultant should also assess less obvious means of communication, from the impact of architecture to the way the telephones are answered.

4. The communications audit is concerned both with the logic and quality of all communications.

References

[1] Maxwell Hutchinson, 'Three Minute Culture: Architecture', with Maxwell Hutchinson and Michael Ignatieff on BBC TV, 1989

6

THE CORPORATE IMAGE

Having assessed the challenges facing an organization and the strategy it has developed to meet them, the strengths and weaknesses of the corporate image now need to be assessed. Here we are concerned with the perceptions of a company's various audiences. Fundamentally, we are looking at whether these perceptions will help the achievement of the strategy or whether they will hinder it. Indeed, we should look to see whether the strategy itself is recognized and understood by the company's internal and external audiences.

Inevitably, this process of analysing an organization's image is complex. Typically, it would involve several months' work and, in the case of a major multinational, it could take years. The requisite information is obtained through an interview programme, which includes both group discussions and face-to-face interviews. This would encompass a variety of audiences from consumers, suppliers and shareholders to employees.

The scope of this phase can be considerable. In a recent study of this type for a Polytechnic, it included academic administrators, lecturers, competitive academic organizations, local businesses using research resources, businesses using conference facilities, past and future employers of graduates, teachers in schools, local education authority advisers, journalists, educational researchers, educational inspectors, past and present students (in groups), school leavers and parents. However, for our purposes, the audiences can be broken down into a limited number of groups. (Figure 7).

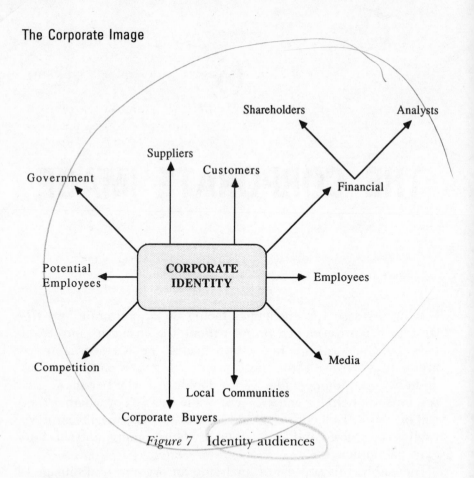

Figure 7 Identity audiences

Employees

Most corporate strategy statements never actually penetrate
the ranks of management to touch the minds and imagina-
tions of the employees doing the everyday work of a company.
Yet they are the people facing customers and clients daily and
for good or ill, creating the true image and reputation of the
business ... If your employees don't know what the strategy
of the business is, or can't translate it into workable terms, the
strategy will simply grind into oblivion somewhere in the
offices of senior management.[1]

The internal audience of an organization is often the most
important audience of an identity programme. It is the employees
who will determine whether an organization is able to meet its
objectives or not. It is the employees who will determine the

product quality. And it is the employees who will determine the corporate image.

The value of employee endorsement of and commitment to corporate objectives is nowhere better illustrated than in Robert Guest's classic article 'Managerial Succession in Complex Organizations', which was published in the *American Journal of Sociology* in 1962. The article compared two studies on the impact of managerial succession:

- Alvin W Gouldner's study of a gypsum plant;[2]

- Guest's own study of what is generally reckoned to be a General Motors plant.[3]

The studies both concern themselves with what happens in organizations when a new leader is introduced.

The studies

In Gouldner's case study, the introduction of a new leader in the gypsum plant resulted in a rapid increase in managerial/employee tension. In Guest's study, a previously acrimonious relationship was transformed into a stable and motivated environment. The differences in the two management approaches were various and we do not need to concern ourselves with all of them here. The interesting facet of the study from our point of view is the different attitudes to communication.

In the Gouldner study the new manager saw communications as a means of carrying up information and carrying down policies and orders. There is nothing fundamentally wrong with this, if the strategic communication takes account of the prevailing identity of the organization. Employees will understand the corporate direction and will be able to translate it into workable terms. In this instance however, the new manager took no account of the corporate identity and sought to undermine it. As Gouldner points out: 'It is difficult to maintain, and especially to create, informal solidarity in pursuit of ends which are so differently valued by group members.'

In contrast, the manager of the automotive plant, who was given the pseudonym of Cooley, took the trouble to understand

the identity of the organization and used inter-active communications to stimulate employee ownership of ideas:

> In his early period in office Cooley met regularly with his
> immediate staff. The purpose of these meetings was not to
> relay pressure down from the corporate organization, but
> rather to encourage ideas from below which had been with-
> held previously. In time and without the manager's directing
> the action, similar meetings 'sprang up' at all levels and
> departments. The manifest purpose of the group meetings
> was to solve 'business' problems, yet the experience had
> unanticipated consequences. Each member gained a feeling
> of reinforcement and support not provided for in the formal
> 'scalar' relationships.[4]

Cooley managed to transform his plant from the poorest per-
former in the group, across a number of indicators, to the best,
while the manager of the gypsum plant had to be removed from
his job to try to reduce tensions. This study demonstrates two
things:

- Firstly, it is important to communicate direction to employees.

- Secondly, that direction and its communication have to take
  account of the realities of the corporate identity.

Interviews

If we recognize the value of these two functions, the problem is
how to understand employee perceptions of the organization they
work for. This is normally achieved by a number of semi-
structured depth interviews. The number of interviews required
will vary enormously and is dependent on the nature of the
problem and the complexity of the organizational structure. It
may be a few dozen, it may be several hundred. There are no
hard and fast rules, it is a question of judgement.

Again, with the interview structure, there can be no easy
formulas. The interview should probe those areas that are found
to be important from the earlier stages of analysis. However,
there is one broad dictum: concentrate on whether the strategy is
understood by employees and whether it is compatible with their

perceptions of the organization and workable within their frame of reference.

The permutations of communication success or failure are several:

- The strategy as defined by senior management is understood by employees, but as the Gouldner case study demonstrated, incompatible with their understanding of the organization.

- The strategy is understood, compatible, but employees have not been given the tools to translate it into reality.

- The strategy is not communicated.

- The optimal — the strategy is communicated, compatible and workable.

We will have seen in the communications audit the means by which management communicate with employees, both in an overt sense with newsletters and formal statements of purpose, and also through committees and groups. We will have also observed in our analysis of the identity, the acts and deeds of management that reinforce the strategy and show it in action. The task now is to assess the success of those mechanisms.

3i

A good example of a successful communicator of strategy is the venture capital organization known as 3i. Originally called Finance for Industry, 3i was comprised of four constituent parts: ICFC (finance for small companies); TDC (development capital for small technology-based firms); FFS (finance for shipping); and FCI (finance for large companies.) The problem with this structure was that the company's audiences did not understand how the various companies related to each other, nor the terms of the relationship of the individual companies with Finance for Industry.

In spite of the quite specific remit of the four companies, there was a common strategic focus for all of them: the creative use of money. To bring these companies together the company chose the name Investors in Industry (3i), and developed a branding device which endorsed the idea of creativity (Plate 4). However, if the strategy were to be successful, employees needed to develop a common understanding of what 3i represented. To disseminate the 3i strategy, the company places a strong emphasis on training, and specifically training that promotes using money in creative ways. Similarly, all the communications of the company are impressively distinctive and creative, both in terms of design and language. As an example of the latter, given the background of the organization, there was a tendency to refer to it as an 'institution'. The word is now taboo in 3i communications, as being incompatible with the declared direction of the company. The new strategy was not communicated overnight, but by being consistent it has permeated the whole organization. Wendy Millard of 3i believes: '3i is very keen on training. We try to teach people that you don't work for 3i; you are 3i. If I'm the only 3i person you've met, then your impression of 3i is related to me.'

Although 3i is very successful at communicating its strategy to its employees, much of British and American industry pays only lip-service to it. The Japanese, however, with their tradition of lifetime employment, are singularly adept at creating ownership of a strategy. Describing the typical Japanese employee, Kenichi Ohmae says: 'Because he feels married to the company for life, and believes their fortunes will rise or fall together, he has in a way a top management perspective.'

With a strong sense of cohesion, a Japanese organization can move at one, and move quickly, when a new strategy is determined. With the exception of the few, this is difficult to envisage in most Western companies. The normal attitude is either that internal communications don't really matter, or alternatively that messages are conveyed all the time, but are never truly owned by the employees. Dr Ernest Mario, Chief Executive of Glaxo, sums up his company's stance and also the failings of others:

> I don't think you can build a corporate identity for a group unless you get everyone together and talk to them about what is going on in the company. ... I prefer over-communicating with employees to under-communicating. You need to share information with employees. That is quite different from the way most British and American companies operate.[5]

Horizontal and upward communication

Although the downward flow of information in an organization is vital, the other aspects of horizontal and upward communication must also not be ignored. Indeed, the upward flow of information was one of the purposes of Cooley's meetings. Two things need to happen for successful communication. First, the organization has to have an environment where the free expression of ideas is nurtured. This suggests an identity which places importance on the views of each individual. Secondly, the mechanisms in the form of suggestion boxes, quality circles, meetings, and committees need to be in place to facilitate the communication flow. You cannot have one without the other. Suggestion boxes, for example, will achieve little unless people feel confident that their ideas are valued and will be taken seriously. It is not an uncommon experience to interview managers who assure you that they are good communicators yet know virtually nothing of what their employees think. This is a very obvious limitation for someone developing a corporate strategy and also ignores the huge potential for achieving savings or developing more efficient ways of working.

Kenichi Ohmae cites the savings that Toyota have achieved:

> Toyota's suggestion box, is certainly not unique to Japan. Back in the early 1950s, the company's 45 000 employees turned in only a few hundred suggestions annually. Today, Toyota gets 900 000 proposals — 20 per employee on the average — per year, worth $230 million a year in savings. Even for a company the size of Toyota, that's not an insignificant sum.[6]

In addition to upward communication, the horizontal flow of communication between business units has to be considered. The committees, groups and written communication that go across corporate structures, ensuring that each unit knows what the other is doing and making it possible to exploit areas of interest, while avoiding duplication of effort, is a vital component of corporate strategy. Without the cross-transfer of knowledge, Courtaulds would not have had the necessary skills to develop carbon-fibre (see Chapter 2). Similarly, Sony encourages the cross-fertilization of ideas by a series of committees, so that principles learnt in one technological area can be applied where necessary to another. Porter believes that these inter-relationships can have a great impact on an organization, but all too often they are ignored:

> Strategically important inter-relationships have long been present in many diversified firms. Little attention has been given to identifying and exploiting them systematically, however, and many inter-relationships have remained untapped.[7]

When analysing employee perceptions it is therefore important to ascertain whether the personnel in one business unit understand the perspective of the next. Whether it is important that they should will depend on whether synergy can be achieved by linking the activities of units together in any way.

Consumers

Consumer perceptions can be understood by using both quantitative and qualitative research. However, our prime method of probing attitudes is the use of either one-to-one depth interviews or group discussions.

This qualitative bias to consumer research underlies the fact that unearthing perceptions is not a superficial pastime. We are seeking to understand what consumers really think about a company and its products, whether they detect a certain personality or style in an organization, and whether that organization is understandable in their terms. This requires research to dig deep into consumers' collective perceptions of a company, both in terms of their actual everyday experience of it, and in the communications they receive.

Marks and Spencer

What is it, for example, that determines consumer perceptions of the UK retailer Marks and Spencer? Firstly, it is direct experience of purchasing products, and, traditionally, specific products such as knitwear and underwear. Secondly, it is the sum of received communications in the form of packaging, store environment, sales assistants and product display. Virginia Valentine, of the research company Semiotic Solutions, explains it like this:

For the purposes of understanding corporate imagery, however, it is the way the sign becomes a symbol of the mythologies which guide our deepest and most emotional decisions, which is of the greatest importance.

Perhaps the best example is provided by Marks and Spencer's knickers.

For many years, consumers would talk of the mythologies of value which surround Marks and Spencer as symbolised by knitwear and knickers.

She goes on to make the point that although Marks and Spencer still has strong connotations of value, the symbols of that have changed: 'Now, however, although Marks and Spencer is still surrounded by myths of value, the symbol has shifted from knitwear and knickers to Moules Marinière and Chicken Tikka.'[8]

In the minds of consumers Marks and Spencer gives good value. In reality, its value may be poor outside these areas of strength, and the company has suffered criticism in the recent past about its performance in women's fashion. None the less, the overall positive image remains as long as Marks and Spencer continues to perform in key, frequently-purchased product areas.

Although Marks and Spencer, through its acquisition of Brooks Brothers, could no longer be regarded as having a single unified corporate identity, from the point of view of the UK consumer there is only one Marks and Spencer. There is no confusion as to what Marks and Spencer is and what it does.

In the case of an identity, where the whole focus is on the brand personality, there will probably be little or no consumer perceptions of the corporate personality coming through. This is the way a company such as Unilever likes to keep things.

The potential area of consumer confusion is the company which is a combination of corporate and brand messages. As Wally Olins says: 'The main problem this kind of complex company has to face is the extent to which the imagery of the corporation as a whole obliterates, dominates or is endorsed by its component parts.'[9]

An overall strategic message about a diversified organization may be coming through from its communications, but the organizational structure may blur the meaning in the eyes of the consumer. The corporate branding can get confused with or dominate the business unit branding.

Royal Opera House, Covent Garden

The Royal Opera House in Covent Garden has an image of artistic excellence that ranks it alongside the other great opera houses of the world. Given that it has the word 'opera' in its title, there is a strong perception that the Royal Opera company is one of the three performing companies. However, the two ballet companies: the Royal Ballet and Birmingham Royal Ballet, do not have such a clear association with the Opera House. Thus we have to ask the question 'Is the image of the Royal Opera House so strong as to overwhelm the image of the performing ballet companies?' If we conclude that it is, there may be grounds for developing stronger visual cues that communicate the inherent strength of the Royal and Birmingham Royal Ballet.

The resolution of these types of conflicts will be looked at in Chapter 8. However, we should establish at this stage of consumer research whether the link between parent and brands is clear and whether the right message about the relationship between the two has been conveyed.

The Financial Community

Within this definition I have included all those people or organizations who are interested primarily in the performance of the company at corporate level. These include both individual and institutional shareholders, as well as the market analysts, banks and brokers. The interesting thing for the identity consultant is that the financial community has increasingly become the focus of identity programmes. Given the changing nature of competition, outlined in Chapter 2, perhaps this is not surprising. The number of companies restructuring in response to financial and strategic pressures is considerable, and this is the very occasion when identities rise above the subconscious.

In relative terms, the recognition of the value of communicating with the financial community and creating the right sort of

Plate 1 Bloomsbury

Plate 2 Prudential Corporation

the department for Enterprise

Plate 3   Department for Enterprise

Plate 4   Investors in Industry (3i)

Plate 5   USAir

Plate 6   Gulfstream Aerospace

Original Roundel

As modified – 1969

Plate 7   ICI

The Apple logo is a trademark of Apple Computer, Inc.

Plate 8   Apple

Plate 9   Transamerica

Plate 10   Samaritan — the new graphic

Plate 11   Samaritan — the old graphic

Plate 12   Unisys

Plate 13   Faber

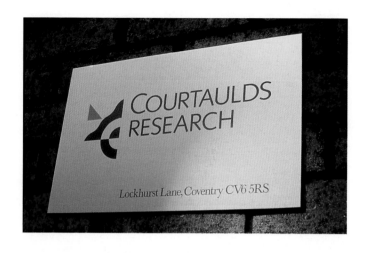

Plate 14   Courtaulds plc

image is new. In the UK, the first takeover to be waged in the media occurred in the mid-1980s when Trafalgar House launched its bid for P&O. Since then companies have increasingly recognized the importance of projecting themselves.

Hanson

One of the best known UK corporate campaigns is Hanson's 1986–8 'Company from over here that is doing rather well over there.' The campaign is well remembered, partly because of its use of humour in delivering detailed company information and partly because it was one of the first examples of corporate image advertising in the UK and paved the way for such subsequent corporate profile raisers as ICI's 'World Class', British Airways winking eye and BOC's pink flamingos. Previously, corporate advertising had either been announcing results or had been linked to takeovers. Indeed the catalyst for the initial phase of Hanson's campaign was a takeover. In December 1985 Hanson launched its bid for Imperial — the tobacco, food and drinks group. The bid was rebuffed and Hanson was on the receiving end of some strong advertising built around the theme of 'famous brands doing famously'. Hanson recognized that it would have to communicate in a more impressive way, so it developed a campaign that clearly conveyed the scale of its operations. However, Imperial capitulated before Hanson could run the campaign. Having seen the way that Imperial's advertising had affected the opinions of shareholders, Hanson decided to run the advertising anyway and in the next two and a half years spent an estimated £8.5 million in national media.

We should note that when an acquisition is an all-cash offer, the perception or image of the acquiring company tends to be less important. Shareholders are fundamentally concerned with the sum they are to realise. However, when the offer involves some form of paper, then the perception of the acquirer is vital. When UDS was under threat from Heron International, Hanson stepped in at the eleventh hour to make an offer to Sir Robert Clark, the UDS chairman, which was rapidly accepted. '"We like Hanson. I don't think there will be any problem about his shares holding their price. He's got a terrific profit record," said Sir Robert.'[10]

In both cases, the image of the acquired matters, because it will determine shareholder loyalty. If a company has clearly and successfully communicated its strategy and its worth to key financial audiences, then the degree of loyalty will tend to be higher. Indeed, the share price itself should be higher as a reflection of the true value of the company, thus acting as a barrier to acquisition. Therefore, there is a clear need to communicate value to investors and analysts.

Hanson is one example of a company that understands the need to communicate to its financial audiences. However, there are many companies who ignore this need, so consequently the image of the company gets out of kilter with the corporate reality. In these days of financial raiders this is obviously a dangerous position. A company which fails to explain the range of its activities and its strategies can all too easily 'come into play'. As Clive Chajet, Chief Executive of identity consultants, Lippincott & Margulies says:

> If you accept the premise that perception is important to the valuation of a stock, and if you also agree that the greater the undervaluation, the more tempting a company is as a takeover target then you must conclude that a good defense against an unwanted takeover would be achieving an accurate and positive perception of the true reality of the company. But it must be warranted. If it's not warranted, it could do double damage.[11]

Quantitative research

As with all research into a company's audiences, a qualitative approach is valid. However, some companies also conduct quantitative work to establish impressions before embarking on one-to-one interviews with analysts or brokers. Indeed it is often the more regular, less in-depth surveys that highlight the image problem in the first instance. The experience of the US foods and distribution company, McKesson, aptly demonstrates this:

> We used to do an annual survey of the opinions of investment analysts about the company. It always came out the same: very few positive comments for the simple reason that the company wasn't doing very well and hadn't done well for four or five years. We were regarded as a kind of sleepy, old, dull company with lacklustre performance, because that's what we were.[12]

What the research aims to determine is whether the image of the company matches up with the identity, the corporate reality. Unfortunately for McKesson, the problem at the time was that the image matched the identity all too closely.

Bausch & Lomb

An example of a company that had changed the reality, but not its image, is Bausch & Lomb. When identity consultants Lippincott & Margulies conducted a programme for the company, they found it was tracked by a small number of analysts in the manufacturing sector. This was not surprising, given the company's heritage as an optical manufacturer, and the preponderance of manufacturing and engineering naming policies. Similarly, the rather awkward corporate structure served to confuse the nature of the company and what it did.

What the company had become, through a series of acquisitions and the adoption of a new strategy, was a service-oriented healthcare organization. To try to correct analyst perceptions, the company began presenting itself as Bausch & Lomb Healthcare and Optics Worldwide. The manufacturing terminology was discarded and now, when the company presents itself to analysts, it breaks down the organizational structure into four major competency areas: personal health; medical; biomedical; and optics. The result has been that the company is now followed by a different and more appropriate set of analysts. However, as Steve Gilliatt of Lippincott & Margulies notes, there have been other benefits: 'For the first time senior management at the company can articulate what the company does in a clear fashion, and I think the success of that is that the stock price of Bausch & Lomb has gone up about 40 per cent in the last six months since the announcement was made.'

Personal contact

Of course, it could be argued that with only a limited number of analysts and institutional investors interested in any one company, a more appropriate approach would be personal contact. This should happen whether a company is looking to wider programmes of communication or not. Regular contact between senior managers and financial audiences is a vital part of the communication process. The second counter-argument is that these financial professionals are primarily interested in the figures.

Both these arguments have only limited validity. Although institutional investors tend to dominate the market, the individual shareholder is still important. In the UK it has been a declared aim of the Conservative Government to broaden the base of share ownership. This has been most notably achieved in the flotation of such companies as British Gas, British Telecom and British Airways. Similarly, in certain companies there is a wide base of employee shareholding. Procter and Gamble, for example, have 28 000 employee shareholders.

The second argument is that financial professionals not only look at the figures, they also assess the identity and strategy of a company to determine how well that company is positioned to cope with the evolution of a particular industry. Therefore, it behoves a company to communicate, on a continuous basis, an accurate and relevant picture of its activities and how it is working to take advantage of the changes in an industry structure.

Sara Lee Corporation

As further evidence of the importance of communicating with all shareholders and analysts, take the example of the US company, Consolidated Foods. If the name sounds bland, that's exactly what the financial community thought. Consolidated Foods Corporation sold Hanes hosiery, Electrolux vacuum cleaners, Fuller brushes, Coach Leatherware, L'Eggs stockings and Sara Lee baked goods.

As the spread of these businesses suggests, the company did more than produce food. Also, the company had a decentralized structure, so it could not be described as 'consolidated'. Therefore, the name was not only bland, but also inappropriate. This helped to ensure that the stock lacked visibility among the financial community. So, with the help of identity consultants, Anspach Grossman Portugal, the company set out to change its name. According to Robert Lauer, Vice-President of Corporate Affairs: 'The real reason we wanted to change our name was to increase the market value of our stock.[13]

The newly-named Sara Lee Corporation seems, in the first instance, more appropriate to the identity of the company, has some personality and also has connotations of quality derived from its best-known brand identity. Secondly, financial analysts now seem to be more aware of the corporation. Research, one year after the introduction of Sara Lee Corporation, showed that awareness of the company increased from 93 to 100 per cent among security analysts, from 82 to 97 per cent among portfolio managers, and from 76 to 100 per cent among the media.

Financial communities in the UK and US

Overall, there seems to be a far greater awareness of the importance of creating a favourable and accurate image of an organization with the financial community in the US than the UK. There are a number of factors behind this. First, quarterly reporting requirements dictate that a company and its assessors are almost continuously aware of its performance. Secondly, shareholders, both as individuals and institutions, seem to rank higher in management's minds in the US. Finally, the threat from financial raiders and arbitrageurs concentrates US management's minds on the value of communications. However, over the last five years, companies in the UK have begun to take more notice of their financial audience.

Suppliers and Buyers

Both the suppliers and buyers of a company's products will have an image of an organization that will affect the buying/selling relationship. In this context it should be made clear that the buyers are not the end consumers of a product, but the organizational buyers who will be buying products from other companies. For all companies this relationship is important and it will relate back to the company's generic strategy. For a company that has a differentiated product, it will be important that suppliers are able to provide the differentiation value. This means that the suppliers of Marks and Spencer food products are able to deliver the right level of quality control at an acceptable price.

Alternatively, a company that pursues a cost leadership approach will have to adopt procurement policies that will ensure that the company is able to purchase at lower cost than its competitors. The basis of the buyer/seller relationship is thus twofold: it is experience and it is also image. J Sainsbury has such a strong reputation as a buying organization, that it is able to purchase products of high quality at low cost. This is facilitated by the company's single unified identity. If the company was highly diversified, and operated under a variety of trading names, those trading companies would not carry the weight that 'J Sainsbury' does. Suppliers would enter the trading relationship with a different set of expectations. There would not be the same image of a powerful monolith.

From the suppliers' point of view the same maxim applies. Appear as a series of small companies and the buying party will sense that it has the balance of power. Convey the organization as a large coherent supplier and the balance of power will tilt. For example, Courtaulds originally used to have a variety of business unit names. However, the company decided, after a lengthy corporate identity review, that it would rename all its units Courtaulds. 'It [the identity programme] has certainly enabled us to explain the spread of our businesses more easily than we could before, both to the City and our big customers.'

With Marks and Spencer buying textiles, floor tiles and packaging materials from Courtaulds, the greater degree of visual cohesion created by the new identity programme allows the links between the operating divisions to be recognized by buyers. This provides the potential for market inter-relationships to be achieved:

> A firm should develop both its corporate identity as well as those of its business units, within the firm and outside. This not only affects management's view of themselves, but can directly facilitate the achievement of market inter-relationships by making buyers more aware of the connection between business units.[14]

The ability to buy effectively and therefore meet strategic needs is important in all industries. However, in automotive manufacturing it is crucial, and this is one of the areas in which the Japanese excel. Traditionally, Western manufacturers have found it harder to get the quality/price level right. This perhaps says something about buying practices, but it also says something about image. If a company establishes an image, backed up by performance, which says that the quality of key components is not that important, this will encourage suppliers to produce to lower specifications.

However, if a company stresses in its actions and its communications that only top quality components are acceptable, the supplier attitude is likely to be different. To reach this stage, it may take some overt signals. The buying company may have to cease doing business with those companies that fail to perform, and make its reasons known by instructing their buyers to tell the story to other suppliers, or by issuing stories to the press. Alternatively, it may have to start rejecting components at a higher rate or begin to impose penalty clauses. In the days prior to privatization, Jaguar's reputation for quality and reliability was appalling. To correct this a rigorous and well-communicated quality regime was initiated. This has helped the company regain its reputation for quality vehicles.

Government

Lobbying

Politicians and civil servants can dramatically influence the well being of companies. This has long been recognized in the US and Europe, and is behind the growth in the political lobbying industry. Even in the UK there is a long history of political lobbying, dating back to the formation in 1839 of the Anti-Corn Law League of Cobden and Bright. They employed the sort of methods which would be familiar with the current day political lobbyists on Capitol Hill. Members of Parliament were pressurized, mass meetings were held, pamphlets were circulated to every elector in the country by the new penny post, and public opinion polls were undertaken. The objective of this activity was to influence the attitudes of the government in their favour.

Today, companies employ lobbyists and PR agencies to try to create a favourable impression of an organization or an industry. Overall, it is difficult for them to influence major policy initiatives, but organizations should try to understand the political environment and communicate effectively with governmental audiences. In the UK, government policies are usually the outcome of departmental conflict within government, as well as pressures from outside. This necessitates communicating to civil service departments as well as MPs. One Labour minister, on first entering government, was surprised at the power of the department, commenting: 'We came briefed by our departments to fight for our departmental budgets, not as Cabinet ministers with a Cabinet view.'

The department in turn faces a series of often conflicting pressure groups. Thus, the Tobacco Advisory Council, a body funded by tobacco manufacturers to create a positive image of the industry, is countered by ASH, who are against the tobacco industry and its policies. Given the continual conflict between these parties, the department gets to know the protagonists and will consult them to determine their reactions and attitudes to policy changes. Although the Thatcher regime changed the consensus-seeking approach to government, the idea of adversarial policy-making remains essentially a myth.

Policy committees

Companies continually need to communicate their identities and their strategies to government. If a positive image can be created, companies have the potential to become part of, or have access to, the relevant policy committees. This enables them to detect the possibility of policy change at an early stage. It will also enable a company to galvanize political opinion behind it in a moment of crisis or a moment of expansion. The latter is especially significant when a company is acquiring overseas and encounters nationalist or strongly regional sentiments, or alternatively, if the acquisition involves any defence issues.

US Congress

In British companies' raids on corporate America, congressmen have consistently stepped in to lobby one way or the other. Although acquisitions are not currently being pursued in the same volume as the late 1980s, it was notable that in the last big, publicly acrimonious takeover battle, politicians intervened between two foreign-owned companies — BAT and Sir James Goldsmith's Hoylake consortium.

Last Thursday, in what was believed to be the first public intervention by North American politicians in a takeover struggle between foreign-owned companies, more than 200 congressmen denounced the bid as a threat to policyholders and to American jobs and they condemned the attempt to sidestep state laws. Goldsmith called the opposition 'yet another tribute to the tentacular lobbying power' of BAT.[15]

The strength of BAT's image in Congress is all the more surprising given the hostility that the company itself faced when it acquired the US insurance company, Farmers.

Local Communities

The development of a positive corporate image with the local community surrounding a head office or a factory can benefit a company in two respects. First, it can help ensure that the company has a respected voice when it wishes to expand, develop a new greenfield area, or even scale down operations.

Secondly, the image of an organization with its local community will in part determine its prospects in employing the best local people.

Both of these factors are accentuated with size. When a company dominates a town, such as Pilkington does at St Helens in Lancashire, or when a company is fundamentally important to the economic vitality of an area, such as Ford is in Detroit, or BP America is in Cleveland, Ohio, then there is a need for a close link to be developed between the company and the community. A company that works hard at promoting a fusion of interests will be better positioned to implement its strategies, especially if the strategy implies local danger, such as with the building of a chemical plant or a nuclear power station or local unemployment.

When Robert Horton took over the role of Chairman of BP America, he noted that 'the person who sits in this office has a tremendous influence on the city' (of Cleveland). Therefore, part of the BP Chairman's role was to communicate clearly the corporate strategy:

Horton's first job in Cleveland was to calm his employees and convince them that the interests of BP and Cleveland coincided. To do so he had to sell BP's US employees on the good sense underlying the BP business strategy, even if the strategy was painful short term.[16]

The Media

The media is an important audience to the extent that the media's image of a company will help determine the image of all the previously cited audiences, as well as a company's competitors. The easiest way to get at journalists' perceptions is to determine who the key industry commentators are and then interview them individually.

The interesting aspect of this phase of research is that well-informed commentators will often have an in-depth and broad ranging view of a company and the industry it competes in. As the receivers of information from an organization they are also ideally placed to pass comment as to whether or not the company is a good communicator.

Traditionally, the advertising agency, Saatchi & Saatchi, has been good at maintaining good and continuous relationships with the marketing media, and has managed to maximize the coverage of its new business gains and campaigns and minimize the coverage of account losses and poor performance. However, it is also worth noting that in recent times the company has been seen to be poor at communicating with its financial audiences.

Given the size and scope of media audiences, the value of a proactive media relations policy cannot be underestimated. Organizations which lack this media orientation often find it surprising that although they have made significant achievements, they gain no media coverage. This opens up the issue of the nature of dissonance between the corporate reality and corporate perceptions.

Dissonance

What we should have gained, through a series of interviews and discussions, is a picture of an organization as it sees itself and as others see it. The task now is to relate the perceptions of the organization back to the corporate reality. This will enable us to define the problems that exist and determine the objectives for the identity programme. Although it is difficult to disassociate the reality from perceptions, we should now have enough information from the identity and image research to determine the positioning of a company in its industry, both as it really is and as it is seen (Figure 8).

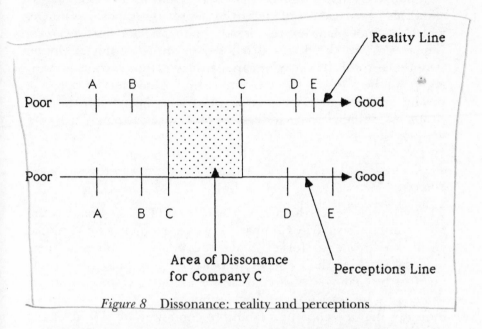

Figure 8 Dissonance: reality and perceptions

This may not, however, be consistent for all audiences. A company may be more adept at communicating with its financial audiences than it is with its employees. Alternatively, one business unit may be good at communicating, while another is not. Thus, having defined an overall corporate positioning map, subsidiary positioning maps need to be drawn for all key audiences and divisions. There are three potential outcomes to this analysis.

Scenario 1

We find that the image and the reality are accurately aligned. In other words, a company has communicated its position and its strategies with all key audiences in a positive way. Thus, the corporate image will help support the corporate strategy.

Scenario 2

We find the image to be significantly better than the reality. This would imply that the company has been effective at communicating a desired image, but that operationally it cannot sustain that position. This is either because the company has not understood its identity, or that it has been suffering from wishful thinking. It could also be due to the vestige of a previously positive image, which has not been entirely lost in spite of poor performance. Jaguar Cars in the 1970s is a good example of this attribute. People were still buying the cars because of the corporate heritage, not because of the current reality. However, although a positive image can carry a company for a short time, the real problems still have to be addressed, otherwise customers will vote with their feet.

Scenario 3

That reality is better than or at least different to the image is the most common scenario. Companies managing their more tangible assets are prone to forget about the intangible ones at their disposal, such as their corporate image. These intangible assets need to be managed if a company is going to communicate its value and its direction to key audiences. A failure to do so indicates that a company is failing to communicate effectively.

● If Scenario 1 exists, there would be no need to alter the communication process. The only check that would have to be made is whether the current presentation of the identity was in any way limiting to future growth.

● Scenario 2 would focus thoughts on operational problems that need to be resolved before addressing any communication problems.

● Finally, Scenario 3 is concerned with the process of communication.

In most companies, we in fact find a mixture of communication and operational problems, and a mixture of different perceptions among different audiences. For example, the UK company Prudential was traditionally known as an insurance company, although by the late 1970s, the company had diversified and become a more broadly based financial services group. Financial analysts were aware of the company's breadth of activities, but research among consumers showed that they still saw the organization primarily as an insurance group. With the liberalization of financial services in the UK market, in the wake of 'big bang', the image and the identity became even more noticeably dissonant. Similarly, within the company, there was a lack of awareness as to the company's activities and the size of its operations. The company had changed significantly, but both employees and consumer perceptions had not kept up with the pace of change. The company had innovative products and high levels of service, but it was seen as solid, almost staid. The launch of the new identity was part of the means of signalling change. Gwes Lloyd of Prudential summarizes the benefits:

> For the first time the staff realized what the Prudential was and that it was an international organization. There were quite senior people who didn't really realize the size of the organization. In going through the process of corporate identity this breadth of financial services came out. We were signalling that we had changed and that we were capable of keeping the pace going.

Once we have understood the nature of a company's identity, the source of its uniqueness and also its sense of direction, we can determine whether the existing image of the company accurately reflects its essential attributes, and whether this image will help the company achieve its future strategies. If the problems are reality driven, then the operational problems have to be addressed, because communicating an inaccurate or falsely optimistic picture of an organization cannot only be misplaced, but positively detrimental. If the problems are connected with perceptions, then it is communications that have to be addressed. Having defined the problem, the priorities now need to be set and the objectives of the identity programme clearly determined.

Summary

1. A company has a great diversity of audiences, all of whom will form an image of that company from the communications they receive.

2. The audiences include employees, consumers, market analysts, investors, bankers, suppliers and buyers, government, the local community, and the media.

3. The image can be assessed by a series of one-to-one or group interviews. It can then be compared to the reality of corporate performance, to ascertain whether the image is helping or hindering the achievement of corporate goals.

4. If the image is significantly better than the reality, this implies an operational problem; if the reality is better than the image, this implies a communication problem. Companies are often a mixture of the two and this will need to be taken into account when the final objectives of the identity programme are set.

References

[1] David Drennan, 'Down the Organization', *Management Today* (June 1988)

[2] Alvin Gouldner, *Patterns of Industrial Bureaucracy*, (Free Press of Glencoe, 1954)

[3] Robert Guest, *Organizational Change: The Effect of Successful Leadership* (Richard D Irwin Inc, 1962)

[4] Robert Guest, 'Managerial Succession in Complex Organisations', *American Journal of Sociology*, **68**, (1962)

[5] Gareth David, 'New Glaxo Chief has a Blue Chip Policy for Future', *The Sunday Times* (24 September 1989)

[6] Kenichi Ohmae, *The Mind of the Strategist*, (Penguin, 1983) p 207

[7] Michael Porter, *Competitive Advantage* (The Free Press, 1985) p 319

[8] Virginia Valentine, 'Signs and Symbols', *Survey* (Winter 1988)

[9] Wally Olins, *The Corporate Personality*, (The Design Council, 1978)

[10] Ivan Fallon and James Srodes, *Takeovers* (Hamish Hamilton, 1987) p 127

[11] Clive Chajet, *Sense 88*, (Lippincott & Margulies, 1986)

[12] Neil Harlan-McKesson, *The Corporate Name: Asset or Liability?* (Anspach Grossman Portugal)

[13] Bruce Campbell, *Working Woman* (September 1986)

[14] Michael Porter, *Competitive Advantage* (The Free Press, 1985) p 408

[15] *The Sunday Times* (13 August 1989) section D, p 7

[16] Timothy Harris, 'BP USA', *Management Today* (May 1988)

PART III
THE CORPORATE
IDENTITY PROGRAMME

At any point in time an organization's identity may be entirely in keeping with the corporate strategy and the structure of its industry. As an industry evolves, the strategy of the organization will be adapted to new requirements, so its identity will change almost imperceptibly. However, this process of evolutionary change can be undermined: an organization can get its strategy wrong, necessitating drastic action further down the line to get it back into a successful position, or an industry, or an organization's position within it, can change in a significant way, thus altering the way a company competes. For example, this can happen in a sudden manner in the drugs industry where a successful product can make or break a company.

When the change is evolutionary there is likely to be only limited pressure on an organization to look at its identity. There seems to be a propensity in most organizations for self adjustment. However, if the cumulated effect of change is such that the identity gets out of tune with perceptions, there may be a need for remedial work on the way the identity is presented.

The alternative scenario to evolution is the case of radical change. The problem here is that if a company adopts a strategy that implies a significant departure from what has existed before, there will be a major impact on the elements of the identity. It is impossible, for example, to move from a differentiated company to a low-cost producer without implications for the corporate structure, the type of people and the skills required, the operating and checking systems and the very style of the operation. As Porter says:

> The generic strategies also imply differing organizational arrangements, control procedures and inventive systems. ...
> The generic strategies may also require different styles of leadership and can translate into very different corporate cultures and atmospheres. Different sorts of people will be attracted.[1]

Whether an accumulation of evolutionary change or a sudden radical change is the catalyst, companies come to the point where there is a need to signal a new direction or commitment to both internal and external audiences. When this is reached the presentation of the organization comes under review. Utilizing the research gained from the analysis of the corporate identity and image, an organization, normally in conjunction with a consultant, develops a corporate identity programme. In the next four chapters we will look at the process of communicating the organizational identity through such a programme.

References

[1] Michael Porter, *Competitive Strategy* (The Free Press, 1980), pp 40–41

7

SETTING THE OBJECTIVES

Having gone through what can often be a very lengthy analysis of an organization, we arrive at a point where the objectives of the identity programme need to be determined and agreed by all parties. This is most important because when the identity programme is complete and implemented it must be judged against what it set out to do in the first place. Failure to agree clear objectives can result in acrimony later on.

Before proceeding, however, it should be noted that although I am suggesting that the process of setting objectives comes after a study of the corporate identity and image, in some cases objectives will be set before the initial analysis. This would be the case, for example, if a company was in the process of making an acquisition, and was using an identity programme as part of its strategy to help merge together two very different organizations. The identity programme would then have a very precise role which could be defined at the beginning. The more frequent scenario is that a change in the nature of a company's business, or its operating environment, causes an organization to review the way it does things. This will result in a decision to look at the identity with a broad objective in mind, such as to improve the image of the company. However, when the process described in Chapters 3 to 6 is complete, the objectives will then need to be made more specific and accountable.

Refining Objectives

As an illustration of this refining of objectives, International Harvester originally called in the corporate identity consultants Anspach Grossman Portugal, because they believed they needed someone creative to come up with a name for their operations. Thus, there was a very broad objective in the first instance. After Anspach had completed their interview programme with employees, bankers, security analysts, customers, and managers, it became apparent that the International Harvester name was a liability. Thus, a more precise objective was set after the interview programme: to create a new name that would make a complete break with the past and would indicate the company's new sense of strategic direction. Donald D Lennox, then CEO of International Harvester, describes it thus:

> I didn't see the value of the extent of the research at first. But when I started to see some of the reactions that the Wall Street analysts, the lenders, and some of the vendors had to the old IH, I realized we did have to make a complete break with the past. I learned from this that if you are an old line company with a name that's recognized readily, you can't necessarily assume it is also a greatly respected name.[1]

The important attribute of any communication objective is that it helps fulfil the corporate strategy, and that it works within the constraints set by the nature of the organizational identity. The objectives should set out in some detail the tasks of the identity programme, and — given the size and lengthy time-scale of some programmes — a set of priorities. They should also define the role for corporate communications within the total corporate strategy.

Defining Terms of Reference

In Chapter 1 definitions of identity, image and communications are set out. However, they are not the only definitions around, and when the communication objectives are set it is best that the identity consultant and the client company check they are speaking the same language. Objective setting also needs to clarify the intended scope of the programme. The identity consultancy has to know what is possible, what is within their remit and what other programmes of change may be running at the same time as the identity programme. This is the time for honesty. The client company may undermine the effectiveness of the relationship with the consultancy if secrets are kept or support is not whole-hearted.

The consultancy must also be honest in its assessment of what corporate identity can and cannot do. Both in the US and the UK, previous client experience of running an identity review is rare. Without this experience the onus is on the consultancy to avoid over-estimating the capabilities of an identity programme. The consultancy should set out and agree the way the programme will be conducted, the time-scales that will apply, and the areas in which the programme may have implications over and beyond communications.

From the study of the dissonance between the image of an organization and its identity, the nature of communication and operational problems should have been determined already. Thus, the operational problems that will need to be addressed by the company, if they are not to limit the effectiveness of the communications programme, need to be agreed. For example, there is little point in setting communication objectives that are primarily concerned with presenting a company as customer-friendly, if operationally the company pays little attention to its customers. Corporate communications and corporate reality need to be aligned.

Types of Objectives

The communication objectives need to be consistent with the corporate strategy, to take account of the corporate identity and to be achievable within the budgets available. Ideally, they should also have timings attached and be quantified wherever possible. All objectives should be derived from the analysis of the corporate identity and image.

Improving internal communications

Improving internal communications is difficult to quantify, although it is possible to measure whether corporate strategies are understood by use of employee questionnaires. From the image research conducted in the form of one-to-one depth interviews we should also be able to judge the effectiveness of the communication flows from management down and employees up, as well as across divisions. Internal communications may not be the main priority of many identity programmes, but it is an issue in almost all of them. The reality is that management rarely communicate to their employees as well as they think they do.

Heightening corporate awareness

All a company's audiences can be assessed through quantitative research to determine whether they have heard of an organization, how they have heard of it and what they think of it. By looking at the trends and by comparing the client company's awareness figure with those of the competition, norms can be set against which future advancement (or decline), can be measured.

These pre- and post-identity measurements are of the type used by Sara Lee Corporation in the assessment of their profile with the financial community before and after their change of name. The limitation with awareness studies is that many factors other than the identity programme will influence the profile of a company, so it is difficult to directly link an identity programme with movement in awareness data.

Improving the stock price

Improving the stock price is a much more frequent objective in the US than the UK. Companies such as Bausch & Lomb, Beatrice and Sara Lee all initiated identity reviews with the primary objective of improving their position on the stock market. Consequently, their key audiences were all financial. Movement in stock price is also very measurable, but like awareness, directly associating the identity programme to this movement is difficult.

Communicating new strategies

When a company embarks on a new strategy it may find its sense of direction blocked by a wrong or dated impression of the organization. The need to signal change and to indicate a new approach is probably the most frequent catalyst of identity programmes.

This was very much the rationale behind ICI's identity revamp. After the company's disastrous years in the early 1980s, ICI's business focus had moved away from commodity products towards value added items. However, the change was not widely recognized by either internal or external audiences. Being known as Imperial Chemical Industries simply endorsed the old image of the company. As part of the process of updating its image, the ICI roundel was amended, the words 'World Class' were added and the name ICI was formally adopted. Again, the impact of this change can be measured by awareness studies, and by probing an individual's feelings about a company through group discussions.

Providing the flexibility for growth

Some companies find their plans for growth limited by an inflexible name or structure. An extreme example would be BET, which was previously British Election Traction — rather a limitation for a company involved with office services. Similarly, in the US, deregulation in the banking industry has caused many state and city banks to look at their naming policies. The best-known example of this is the now internationally-oriented Citibank, which was previously known as First National City Bank of New York.

Companies may also find that they have worked so hard to communicate a particular position, such as being the lowest cost supplier, that when they want to move into a more upmarket differentiated position, there is a lack of credibility with consumers. In this case, the branding policy needs to be reviewed to determine whether the corporate name needs to be changed, or whether a sub-brand needs to be developed.

Integrating two companies

Unisys is a company that used a corporate identity programme to help integrate the two very different cultures of Sperry Univac and Burroughs. Corporate identity, along with other integration programmes, can help to build a sense of shared values and a commitment towards a new common goal. This is done not only by signalling a common style through overt communications, but also by presenting a clear picture of the organizational structure and how business units and individuals fit into that structure. The role of the identity programme in integration cannot really be measured, but the benefits can be felt.

Creating goodwill

Goodwill is the premium over and above the value of the tangible asset base of a company. This is relevant in the case of an acquisition or merger, because the premium will have to be paid by the acquirer to gain control of a company. What determines the size of the premium is the compensation that needs to be paid to shareholders for their surrender of a future income stream. Shareholders' willingness to surrender those streams will be based on their perception of the corporate body and its associated brands; of both current and future performance. Thus, it is a viable, if difficult to measure, objective for a company to enhance its goodwill, as a defence against acquisition.

Resolving brand structures

One key objective for corporate identity programmes in all companies that have more than one business unit is to present the corporate, divisional and brand structure of an organization so that it is coherent and easily understood by key audiences. Additionally, the degree to which the identities of the component parts of the organization are linked to or isolated from each other needs to be resolved. The guiding principle in this should of course be that whatever best serves the strategy also best serves the visual structure.

Defining the overall positioning

The last, and indeed the most important, objective in any programme is to define the overall identity of the company. Normally this can be summarized in a single positioning statement which is determined by the key point of uniqueness that gives a company its competitive advantage. The positioning will be derived from the company's generic strategy, but it will be more precise as a result of the detailed analysis of the corporate identity. This objective will apply to all identity programmes. Whatever subsidiary objectives have been defined, the positioning statement should guide all an organization's activities, both now and in the future. The positioning statement is thus the embodiment of the identity and that which helps to guide its future evolution. There are three points about the positioning statement which should be noted:

- the positioning must be forward looking and have long term goals;

- the positioning must avoid platitudes;

- the positioning must be single-minded and all encompassing.

Objectives and Audiences

Once we have researched the attitudes of all an organization's audiences, we will almost certainly find that there are different objectives for different audiences. This is not to promote the idea of creating a communications plan which sends out contradictory messages and thereby creates confusion. It is more a question of stressing one aspect of an organizational identity rather than another. For example, if we want to stress the financial perform- ance of the parent company to shareholders, the objective and the communication strategy would be different to the desire to promote the organization as a high technology organization to buyers and suppliers.

For example, Pepsico operates a policy of letting its brands, such as Pepsi-Cola, Frito-Lay, Kentucky Fried Chicken, Pizza Hut, and Taco Bell, be the heroes when it is talking to consumers. However, when the company wants to lobby Washington, it needs to convey the scale of its operations. Thus, its communication objectives to a government audience are different to those to a consumer audience:

There's one audience that we want to make sure understands the total size and scope of our operations: the elected officials in Washington. So the one letterhead that carries all five of our logos is our government stationery. That's an area where strong brand identification really does mean something.[2]

To ensure that objectives are tailored to specific audiences, they should be listed, with objectives attached and then checked for compatibility. For example:

Employees	Improve internal communications
Consumers	Enhance awareness of company and products
Financial	Communicate new strategy and financial performance
Suppliers	Communicate commitment to quality
Buyers	Communicate scope of operations
Government	Influence legislation
Local communities	Communicate new strategy and commitment to expansion
The media	Communicate new strategy and performance

Summary

1. After the analytical phase the precise objectives of the identity programme need to be agreed.

2. Objectives should be set out in detail and timings and priorities attached.

3. Improving internal communications ends up being an objective in nearly all identity programmes, for the simple reason that companies rarely communicate with their staff as well as they think they do.

4. In addition to any other objectives that may be set, an overall positioning statement should be defined to act as a guide for all future actions.

5. Different audiences will have different objectives. These should be specified in turn and then checked to ensure that they are not mutually exclusive.

References

[1] Donald D Lennox (**Navistar International Corporation**), *The Corporate Name: Asset or Liability?* (Anspach Grossman Portugal, 1987)
[2] D Wayne Calloway (Pepsico Inc), *Scene 90* (Lippincott & Margulies, 1988)

8

THE IMPORTANCE OF STRUCTURES

When companies have a simple organizational structure, the main role of a corporate identity programme is to determine the style of an organization and to convey it through a proactive approach to communications. When structures become more complex, an identity programme not only has to determine the style of a number of potentially disparate operations, it also has to ensure that the correct balance between the parent's identity and those of the individual operating units and their brands is presented. The correct balance will be determined by the source of an organization's competitive advantage. In this chapter we will look at the presentation of the organizational structure.

Three Visual Structures

The visual structure is that which is presented to the out-side world. It shows the inter-relationships between the various branded elements of the organization and can vary in a number of ways. Figure 9 shows three basic types of structure: the unitary identity; the branded identity; and the diversified identity. These structures are determined by historical circumstance, by the choice of strategy, and by the elasticity of the company's brand names.

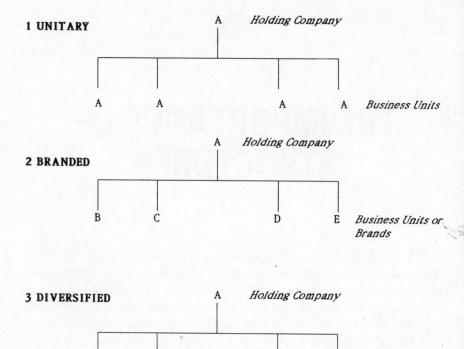

Figure 9 Three types of identity programme

The unitary identity

This is where an organization adopts one name throughout its structure. This tends to be either because the company is new, operates within a tightly defined product area, or the overall corporate name has considerable goodwill and elasticity. Companies of this type tend also to have grown organically rather than through acquisition, although exceptions do exist. (Renault has a unitary identity, yet part of its growth has been fuelled by acquiring companies such as Saviem, Berliet and Dodge.) In the UK, unitary branding tends to appear most commonly among major retailers such as Marks and Spencer and J Sainsbury. However, it is the major Japanese manufacturers who have really understood the importance of building businesses around consumer-oriented themes, that have some of the strongest unitary identities. Their brand elasticity is considerable. A company such as Yamaha operates in a wide variety of leisure markets, from pianos and tennis rackets to boats. Their strategy is consistent in all these markets, as is their branding:

> Genichi Kawakami, rebuilder of Yamaha, makes clear in his autobiography that he made up his mind during a trip to the United States just after the War to develop leisure industries in Japan. Looking at Yamaha's current operations, anyone ignorant of this fact might imagine that the company has simply moved in a fairly aimless process of horizontal diversification. ... In fact, all these moves flowed from Mr Kawakami's original definition of his business domain as 'leisure industries'.[1]

The advantage that Yamaha and companies like it accrue is that each product or service that the company introduces has the same endorsement and a head start in building brand awareness. Economies of communication can be achieved because a consistent message about the company can be built up through all brand communication. Also, it should be easier to create a greater sense of cohesion and direction, because the corporate umbrella is the only structure and does not have to fight for allegiance and visibility with unit identities. However, there are inherent problems with this type of approach. First, because the company is directly associated with any new product launches, the pressure to avoid failure can be greater, making companies potentially wary of taking risks. Secondly, the degree of uniformity this structure implies may act as a constraint on managerial innovation.

The branded identity

Here, the company operates through a series of seemingly unrelated brands. This is typical of companies operating in fast moving consumer goods (FMCG). Companies like Unilever and Procter and Gamble separate their corporate personalities from their brands. The advantage is that a company can put competing brands on to the market without the consumer being aware of the fact, thus enabling a company to segment markets to its advantage. Product failures — all too common in FMCG — are not directly associated with the parent. The likelihood of confusion between a powerful brand personality and the corporate personality is reduced, because the brand is allowed to be the hero.

None the less, there are implicit dangers in the branded approach. There are no economies of communication to be had because consumers will not associate one Unilever product with another and there is no goodwill brought to new product launches, since there is no established consumer franchise.

The diversified identity

This identity type is most common among companies who have started off by developing one core brand, and then, through acquisition or new start-ups, have diversified into new areas. The normal structure is for one of the business units to be branded in the same way as the holding group, and the others to be disassociated or linked by an endorsement.

On the plus side is the potential for the company to balance the benefits of a single identity with those derived from the individual operating companies. This provides for a greater degree of flexibility. However, there are negatives in the traditional diversified structure. The holding company, with one set of audiences, tends to get confused with the business unit, with a separate set of audiences. Secondly, the structure is not easily communicated or understood. Finally, there are cases when business units acquired through diversification become treated as second class citizens within the structure.

Resolving the Structure

Organizational structures often grow over a period of time without referring back to the logic of their operational requirements, or the dictates of corporate objectives. Rather, they evolve in response to problems or successes. There also seems to be a tendency to develop structures that suit the workings of the company, but not the consumers of the company's products. Whatever the internal workings of an organizational structure, a company must try to present a structure that supports the source of its competitive advantage. If that advantage is derived primarily from a strong corporate cohesion, the bias should be towards a unitary identity. Alternatively, if the advantage is derived primarily from strong brands or autonomous business units who need to be close to their markets, then a diversified or branded identity should pervade. The unitary identity will be a more likely choice if a company has a consistent set of strategies among its business units. The units then have the potential to benefit by association with each other. The diversified or branded identity would be a more likely choice if a company has dissimilar strategies. To illustrate this we will look at some examples of companies who have changed their visual structures.

USAir

If a company can gain an advantage by linking its brands or divisions together, it should do so. For example, if the size of a company is important to competitive success, a company should try to develop and communicate a homogeneous structure. This is more likely to convey organizational substance, because of the consistent presentation of the corporate name in all spheres of activity.

This situation is found particularly in the airline business. USAir, one of the United States's largest domestic airlines, is typical. The company, which began as a regional carrier, became a major competitor by route expansion and, more importantly, through the acquisition of Pacific Southwest Airways (PSA) and Piedmont. This transformed the organization into one of the nation's largest carriers in terms of passenger boardings. Rather than retain corporate brand names, such as Piedmount and PSA, and segment the market between them, USAir put everything under one name. This allowed economies of communication to be achieved, as only one brand name needed to be supported. Given the scale of the company's visual presence, the economies of communication were considerable if a unified image could be presented on 425 aircraft, 14 000 ground vehicles and signage in 132 airports, as well as advertising, uniforms, stationery, aircraft interiors and ticket jackets.

The new stature of the airline was further endorsed by the graphics and colour scheme developed by the identity consultants SBG Partners. The corporate colours of red, white and blue, which echo the national flag, clearly endorse the company's position as *the* US carrier (Plate 5).

125

Courtaulds

A similar case is Courtaulds, the British manufacturing group. Originally a textiles company, Courtaulds had grown both organically and through acquisition into a diversified company with 6 operating divisions and 18 business groups in such areas as paints, coatings, adhesives and packaging materials. Diversification was strategically important because the decline in the UK textiles industry had seen the rapid closure of a number of mills and factories in the 1970s. Inevitably, the closures had created a negative image for the company.

In confronting the collection of company names within the group, the identity analysts could again go one of two ways. The names of the acquired companies, some of which had a strong reputation in the market, could be the main focus of the identity programme, which would allow Courtaulds to exploit the strength of such company names as International Paints, a leading manufacturer of marine paints.

Alternatively, to correct the widely held, but inaccurate, perception of Courtaulds as just a textile company, and to convey the central corporate purpose, the identity programme could be weighted towards the corporate.

Courtaulds chose the latter. Company names such as International Paints were sacrificed in the process of renaming everything as Courtaulds and the six divisions became:

- Courtaulds Fibres;

- Courtaulds Woodpulp;

- Courtaulds Chemicals & Materials;

- Courtaulds Coatings;

- Courtaulds Films & Packaging;

- Courtaulds Textiles.*

* Courtaulds Textiles has since become a separately listed plc.

The common naming policy was held to be important by the group, in its efforts to create greater communication and co-operation across the corporate divisions and business groups, as well as in conveying to its key customers that Courtaulds was an international company of stature.

However, in an attempt to signify the individuality of the business units and provide them with their own identities, the corporate logo was colour-coded to distinguish the component parts of the company from one another.

Unitary identities and financial audiences

Already an issue in the US, and becoming one in the UK, is whether these more corporate weighted identities positively influence the image of the company among its financial audiences. Although there is little statistical evidence to support the argument, it seems logical that a company should benefit as the relationship of the parent company is more overtly linked with its subsidiaries. If the company performs well this should have a positive effect on the corporate image among these audiences. However, if performances begin to falter the opposite is true.

Courtaulds now find that when they close down an operation, it is patently obvious to both employees and the City who the parent company is. Before the identity programme, Courtaulds could claim that divisional factories in some parts of the world were not even aware of other division's factories in the same country. This was a rather obvious limitation to exploring the potential for co-operation across the corporate struture, but rather a good way of disassociating the parent company from bad news!

A more subtle balance

The balancing of structures has been presented in stark terms in the previous examples, but in reality the balance may be more subtle. Sometimes the elasticity of the corporate name cannot stretch across all business units, or is inappropriate in some business areas. As Nigel Thomas of the design consultants Fitch says, you have to decide 'whether you can put something famous in engineering on to pig farming'. If the company determines that it cannot, then the pig farming division may have to be separated out as a brand name.

When Midland Bank approached this problem it determined to name most operations Midland. However, the company also owned Thomas Cook, which had an extremely strong brand heritage. Rather than rename the company Midland Travel, the Cook branding was retained, with the endorsement that it was part of the Midland Group of companies.

Similarly, when Chrysler reviewed its identity, it was felt that the heritage of the Chrysler name would benefit the operating divisions. Consequently, within the Chrysler Corporation there are now three product areas:

- Chrysler Motors;
- Chrysler Financial;
- Chrysler Technologies.

These are then further sub-divided (Figure 10).

This weighting towards the corporate is beneficial in communicating the size and scope of the organization to the investment community. However, such is the strength of some of the company's brands, that names such as Gulfstream, the business jet manufacturer, have been retained. The link with the parent company is conveyed, but in a less dominant way, by the words 'A Chrysler Company' on all communications (Plate 6).

Even if a company has determined that it has a series of business activities with like-minded strategies which would benefit from a unitary visual structure, both the positives and negatives of associating each division and brand with each other needs to be determined. The task is, on the one hand, to create a balance between the individual needs of each division to communicate what they do and effectively sell their brands, and, on the other hand, for the organization as a whole to establish a clear position in the market-place.

Although there has been a tendency for companies to opt for unitary structures because of the benefits of economies of communication and single-minded structures, the implications of losing a valued brand name have to be considered. Potentially, this not only comprises the loss of a customer franchise, but as

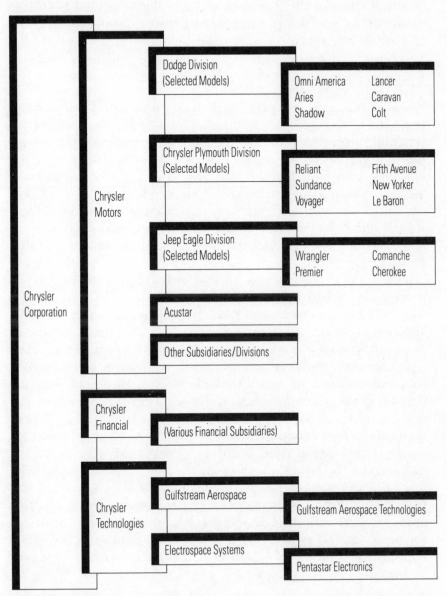

As of January 1990, Chrysler Corporation has changed its structure. This move is for tax and legal reasons and has not impinged on the company's internal or external operations.

Figure 10   **The structure of the Chrysler Corporation**

companies have begun to value brands more highly in assessing the worth of an organization, it may also involve a loss in the eyes of the financial community. The following are some examples of companies who have opted for more decentralized visual structures.

Kingfisher

When companies are presented with the dilemma of how to present a diversified identity, the temptation has been to opt for renaming everything under one corporate umbrella. However, the solution has increasingly been to accept the strengths of the business units and their brands, and to give the organization a less-centralized visual structure. This is not so cohesive, but it should stimulate a more market-responsive organization. In this scenario, the diversified structure with its potential for confusion and anomalies, is exchanged for a partially or wholly branded structure.

The most recent example of this in the UK is the change of name of Woolworth plc to Kingfisher plc. Woolworth in the UK was a £310 million buyout in 1982. In addition to owning the F W Woolworth stores, the company has also acquired Comet, an electrical retailer, Superdrug, a chemist, and B&Q, a DIY retailer. This created a problem because Woolworth stores' performance could all too easily be mixed up with Woolworth, the plc's. While this was not a real issue when Woolworth stores represented the majority of turnover and profits, as it did in 1982, it did become important when Woolworth stores' contributions to profits represented only 29 per cent, as it did in 1991–2. (By this time B&Q had become the largest profit contributor at 37 per cent.) Therefore, the stores have retained the name, while the parent has been distinguished by being renamed Kingfisher. However, this approach is rare in the UK and there has been a tendency to opt for more unified structures. In the United States, on the other hand, the acceptance of branded structures is more widespread.

Primerica

One such example of a branded structure is American Can. This blue chip manufacturing organization had gradually diversified

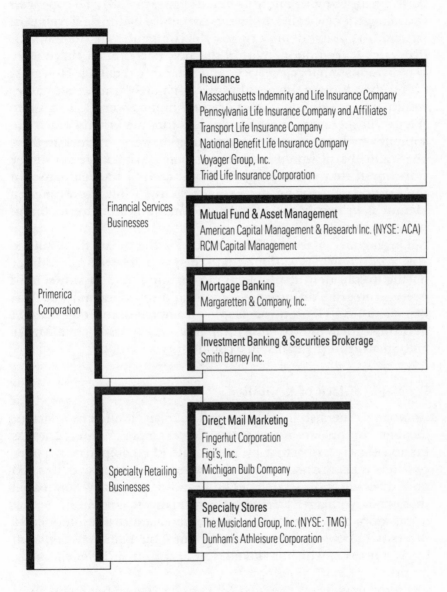

Primerica was recently acquired by Commercial Credit Corp. of Baltimore which then adopted the Primerica name.

Figure 11   The structure of Primerica

out of its packaging heritage to such a point that in the early 1980s it had become a service-based company. In fact the company sold both its name and its interests in packaging in 1981. To cope with this change a new name and a new structure had to be developed. After a corporate identity review the company took the name of Primerica Corporation. Within the new corporation there were two divisions: financial services and speciality retailing. However, rather than impose the new Primerica name on the brand names within the two divisions, the original brands were left in place (Figure 11). The rationale for this was that the brands which the company had acquired through acquisition were so strong in their own right that it would undermine their considerable consumer franchise if they were renamed. Thus, each of the companies in the group has a strong marketing identity, while the Primerica identity is primarily concerned with communicating to the financial community.

The big advantage of this structure is the flexibility it allows. Any acquisition can be slotted into the existing structure, without having to consider the problems of renaming, and the subsequent need to integrate differing corporate cultures. Companies such as Primerica and Hanson can acquire companies and digest them into their corporate structure far more easily than say a Marks and Spencer or a J Sainsbury could.

Problems of lack of flexibility

Companies can also find their strategic plans limited by a lack of flexibility in the naming structure. For example, Tampax Inc was far too closely associated by name with the company's primary product. This became a limitation when the company embarked on a diversification strategy. The brand name totally dominated the corporate image. To enable the company to communicate that it was more than a one product company, and that it intended to diversify into new products, the Tampax Inc name was replaced by Tambrands, which is linked, but also distinct from the main brand.

A similar policy is pursued by Pepsico, where the company is obviously the supplier of Pepsi-Cola and gains by the association with the brand, but is also separate from the brand. In this instance, the brand name is so strong that the image of the brand tends to dominate the corporate, but as D Wayne Calloway notes, this is no bad thing:

> We market Pepsi with a youthful, feisty, aggressive advertising campaign, and we don't mind that kind of image as a company. So instead of the corporate image working its way down, in this case the brand image works its way up.[2]

Such is the strength of the Pepsico portfolio of brands (Frito-Lay, Pepsi-Cola, Kentucky Fried Chicken, Pizza Hut and Taco Bell), and the size of the marketing support behind them, they do not need the endorsement of a well-known corporation to be successful. Thus the structure is 'branded', although the link between the company's main brand and the corporation is clear. The inherent danger in the Tambrands and Pepsico approach is that the secondary brands tend to get overshadowed by the main product.

Loose-tight properties

Although the most appropriate structure for any organization is that which helps provide competitive advantage, there are occasions when a change in the visual structure can have a potential downside. The best way to approach the downside is first to be aware of it, and then to build in other mechanisms into the corporate plan to enable the negatives to be handled. This is akin to the 'simultaneous loose-tight property' that Peters and Waterman refer to in *In Search of Excellence*: 'The excellent companies are both centralized and decentralized. For the most part, as we have said, they have pushed autonomy down to the shop floor or product development team. On the other hand, they are fanatic centralists around the few core values they hold dear.'[3]

Thus, if a company decides competitive advantage is best gained by moving from a unitary to a branded structure, so that its business units are closer to the market and can develop an identity of their own, then other mechanisms that encourage commitment to the centre need to be developed. Indeed, some companies with very strong corporate values can develop more autonomous operations, because they know it will not fundamentally undermine the overall corporate commitment. Procter and Gamble is an example of a company which operates a branded identity, but retains commitment to the centre.

The process can also work the other way. If a company decides to adopt a unitary identity, so that it can achieve economies of scale, then this does not prevent autonomy being given to the business unit. For example, Boeing has a unitary identity, yet each project manager retains extraordinary autonomy.

What this means is that a company can have it both ways: with corporate cohesion *and* business unit autonomy, if strong identities are developed for both the business unit and the corporate. However, the cohesion and the autonomy have to be managed and it is still possible to get the balance wrong. The current problems of resurgent nationalism in much of Eastern Europe and Yugoslavia stem from the fact that the allegiance to the unit/republic, whether it be ethnically or geographically based, is stronger than any allegiance to the federation/centre.

Choosing a Structure

The following 12 points demonstrate which structures are appropriate for which companies:

- Companies with strong brand names, which have significant levels of marketing support behind them, tend to prefer more branded structures.

- Companies with a number of small brands can benefit more from a more corporate approach, where the corporate umbrella lends weight and credibility to the brand.

- Frequently purchased items, typically in the FMCG area, are bought on the strength of the product, therefore the corporate name is relatively less important.

- Major infrequent purchases need the reassurance of a stable, well-known company. This encourages a more corporate weighted structure.

- Companies whose main competitive advantage lies in their financial controls tend to have branded structures.

- In markets where economies of scale are critical to competitive success, such as airline manufacture, there is more to be gained from a single-minded corporate weighted structure.

- Where companies operate within a narrow band of products or markets, it is easier to stretch the brand name across all activities.

- When companies operate in dissimilar markets or have different generic strategies, there will be a tendency to opt for branded structures.

- Companies who market financial products nearly always employ more corporate structures, because of the importance of trust and security that can be more easily conveyed by a unified structure.

- If a company wants to hide the connection between itself and its brands, because of potential conflicts of interest, then a branded structure is best.

- If a company's brands have a strong image, whereas the corporate image is weak, the brands should dominate.

- If the corporate image is strong, and the brand's weak, the corporate should dominate.

Summary

1. When organizations are large and complex, one of the tasks of a corporate identity programme is to determine the correct balance between the parent company, the business units and the brands. The way these elements are presented is known as the visual structure.

2. It is important that the structure is logical and understandable by key audiences.

3. The way to determine the right structure is to assess the source of competitive advantage of an organization. Then each division and brand should be analysed to determine whether or not it benefits by linkage with the other component parts of a group.

4. There may be instances when a single consistent identity is beneficial, such as when significant economies of communication and scale can be achieved.

5. However, if there are valid reasons for excluding a division or a brand from a unitary identity, then the system should be sufficiently flexible to allow for this.

6. Diversified structures can present a problem because the parent company becomes too closely associated with one of its business units.

7. Generally, branded structures are more appropriate when the source of a company's strengths lies in its brands.

8. If the strategy dictates one type of structure, then other mechanisms can be built in to counter-balance the implications.

References

[1] Kenichi Ohmae, *The Mind of the Strategist,* (Penguin, 1983) pp 243–4

[2] D Wayne Calloway (Pepsico Inc), *Scene 90* (Lippincott & Margulies, 1988)

[3] Thomas J Peters and Robert H Waterman Jr, *In Search of Excellence: Lessons from America's Best-Run Companies* (Harper and Row, 1982) p 15

9

THE DESIGN SYSTEM

Having determined the type of corporate structure that best fits the strategy, it now needs to be communicated through the design process. The design aspect of corporate identity programmes has a tendency to be over-stated, primarily because the corporate identity industry has evolved out of the design industry. Business and design journalists have also exacerbated the problem by focusing on the logo as the embodiment of identity programmes. In so doing they have ignored the strategic issues. For example, ICI's new visual identity was pilloried in the press, because the cost of straightening out the wave lines and making marginal type changes was reputed to have cost in the region of £1 million (Plate 7). As Wolff Olins pointed out, what ICI in fact got was something more than a logo:

> A presentation of the company as a series of discrete divisions rather than one amorphous conglomerate, a system for fitting new acquisitions into the structure, a new design style and a strategy for its implementation in 150 countries.[1]

Nonetheless, design does have a role to play in an identity programme, but that role has to be clearly defined.

The Role of Design

The primary role for design in corporate identity programmes is to communicate the identity. This is a view of design that is more than just concerned with aesthetics: it is design as a marketing tool. A design system can:

- define the type of company and what it does;
- indicate the style of a company;
- differentiate a company from its competitors;
- convey the logic of the corporate structure by emphasizing one element at the expense of another; and
- communicate change.

What it does

Normally, when the communications audit is conducted there is a surprising number of ways in which the very name of a company and the descriptions of its activities are presented. A lack of cohesion in this area has enormous potential for creating confusion. Practically speaking, a company name and its descriptor should present within a consistent framework the essence of the company's activities. These descriptors should be 'consumer' oriented. A company's audiences have to be able to relate to the names and the chosen descriptions. However, remembering the need to be strategically responsible, they should not distort the company's activities by claiming to be international when they are not, or to be a consultancy when the company is a manufacturer. Rather, it should be an accurate reflection of what the company does or intends to do. *Clarity* has to be the first objective of any design system.

The corporate style

It is no coincidence that a design consultancy's visual presentation tends to be more creative than that of an accountancy firm or an investment bank. Creativity is at the heart of what a design consultancy does. Although creativity may come into accountancy or investment banking, it is not the lifestyle that this type of company wants to display. Trust, experience and professionalism are more common descriptors of what these types of companies seek to convey. However, as was made clear at the beginning of this book, if the design consultancy fails to deliver creatively, a creative typeface will not correct the situation. Lifestyle has to be supported by performance.

Differentiation

As companies and products find it increasingly difficult to distinguish themselves from each other by their product offering, so design has become an increasingly important weapon. In supermarket retailing, it is very difficult to be distinctive in the product offering. However, design in the form of own label packaging, signage, interior environments, and external communications can help to create a specific and distinctive image of an organization. Also, given the huge volumes of visual messages we are presented with every day, a distinctive approach to design enables a company to stand out from its competitors. Prudential's 'Prudence' (Plate 2) is highly noticeable, while Apple Computers' approach to design helps to create an image of the company that sets it apart from other computer manufacturers (Plate 8).

The Corporate Structure

When the brand name of a company appears alongside the business unit name and/or the corporate name, the relative weight of these components and their inter-relationship needs to be conveyed by their presentation. Even the elements of a company name can be weighted differently to communicate one aspect of a company rather than another. Take the example of Leicester Polytechnic. The word 'Leicester' could be presented with the same weight as 'Polytechnic', or it could be presented as more important, or less. As research indicated that Leicester was well known as a place and had a strong reputation, whereas the word 'Polytechnic' still had connotations as being a second class university, it was decided that emphasis should be given to 'Leicester'. Then, because relationships with the business community tended to be built around academics and schools within the Polytechnic, rather than with the Polytechnic *per se*, it was decided that when a school communicated with external audiences the name of the school would overshadow the name of the Polytechnic. Thus, the presentation of the structure should be related back to the corporate strategy.

Communicating change

When a company changes its direction, it needs to signal that change both to its employees and to its external audiences. One way of doing this is by changing the design of the logo and the other means of communication. If the design change is radical, this would suggest that the organization had also changed in some radical sense.

The Elements of the Design System

The design system can be broken down into four key elements, all of which inter-relate to make a statement about an organization. These elements are: the naming policies; graphics; slogans; and language.

Names

Once the visual structure of the organization has been determined, the efficacy of the existing names need to be assessed. If the existing names are still appropriate to what the company and its divisions do, then they should be retained. Most company names have some sort of reputation, and have often had considerable sums invested in them. So, unless they are patently wrong or limiting to the corporate strategy, they should not be changed. However, in certain circumstances, name changes have to be considered. We have already seen some examples of this: where the existing name was sold (International Harvester, American Can); where there was confusion between an operating division and the parent company (Woolworth); where the existing name was an inadequate descriptor of the company's activities (Consolidated Foods, British Electric Traction); or, in the case of an acquisition, where it was felt to be important that one company name should not dominate the other (Sperry Univac and Burroughs).

However, if the name has to be changed, how is a new name to be determined? Before embarking on a search for an entirely new name, the first place to look is at the existing portfolio of company and brand names. If a name can be taken or adapted from this source it is likely to have more relevance to a company's audiences and especially its employees than an invented name. Examples of this are:

- Tambrands from Tampax
- Sara Lee Corporation from the brand Sara Lee
- Nikon Corporation from its Nikon brand
- Citibank from the colloquial term for the First National City Bank of New York

However, if the search of the company's portfolio of names reveals nothing that is relevant to the corporate strategy, then a

Key Characteristics	200 Analysts/Brokers	100 Individual Investors
	%	%
Pronounceability	51	50
Indication of a company's business	35	45
Indication of corporate qualities	19	33
Indication of corporate values/goals	16·	32
Indication of corporate audiences	16	38
Meaningful in multiple languages	15	17
Indication of company's regional scope	12	29
No specific/intrinsic meaning	7	8
Indications of origin of the company	6	18

In a survey released in October 1988, Landor Associates found that consumers and the financial community have similar views about what's 'extremely/very important' in a corporate name. Other aspects of the survey revealed that more than a third of the brokers surveyed had difficulty selling stocks with names that are meaningless or uninformative; that 94 per cent of investors are more comfortable with familiar names or names that relate to products and services; and that nearly half the brokers and analysts interviewed felt a change to a readily understandable name had a positive effect on the stock value.

Source: DeNeve, Rose 'Whatever Happened to Corporate Identity' *Print*, May/June 1989.

Figure 12 What's important in a name?

new name is the only course of action left. However, a word of warning should be sounded. In a survey by Landor Associates in the US among individual investors and brokers/analysts (Figure 12), brokers had found it difficult to sell stocks with names that were meaningless or uninformative, and individuals' key criteria were 'pronounceability' and 'indication of a company's business'.

Whether in fact the process of searching for a new name is done by computers or people, there is always an element of judgement in the selection process. Where it starts however, is by looking at the communication objectives that have been set. We have to determine how the company wants to be perceived by its various audiences. To give an example of this, when Burroughs acquired Sperry Univac, it was decided that there would be a complete break with the past, and a new name would be developed that had no link with either company. The communication objective was to signal a new direction. The criteria against which to evaluate the names were as follows:

- The name needed to unify the company's employees.

- The name had to have sufficient authority for a major computer company.

- 60 000 customers needed to be reassured that a unified company would maintain continuity of supply of what had been proprietary architecture — that they were not about to become 'computer orphans'.

To encourage employee involvement a naming competition was held among the employees and, out of 31 000 entries, the name Unisys was adopted.

Once the objectives and the criteria are defined, the normal way of finding a new name is to use a computer to explore variations of word roots. This will provide the basis for a more creative approach to building a name from these roots. Once the name choices have been developed, the process of whittling them down to the final candidates needs to get underway. Anything that fails to meet the objectives can be discarded, as can any word that is difficult to pronounce, or has negative connotations internationally, or among ethnic minorities. The final shortlist should then be subjected to two further tests. Firstly, can it legally be used and registered? As companies register more and more names, not only for their own usage, but in some cases simply to stop a competitor using them, the possibilities become limited.

Secondly, does it communicate what we want it to say? Once the legally possible names have been defined, they should then be researched among consumers and other key audiences to check receptiveness. Once the final name has been chosen, it should be registered immediately.

Graphics

Graphics not only relate to the logo itself, but to the graphic presentation of the whole organization. The graphic system should determine the style of design of corporate literature, of signage, of stationery, and of vehicle liveries. It may involve a corporate typeface, a style of photography, a style of illustration, a style of layout and a range of corporate colours. The key question, as with the naming process, is to determine whether the graphic presentation of the company is in tune with the current strategy. If it is then there should be no need to revamp the visual presentation of the organization. However, unlike the naming process, we do not have to deal in absolutes here. The visual presentation can be changed subtly to reflect the re-orientation of a company. Graphics can be carefully evolved to ensure that the link with the past is always maintained. With a name, this is more difficult. (Tambrands is an example of how this *can* be done.)

Looking at the logo itself, there are many examples of companies who have chosen to adjust rather than change the presentation of their symbols. Invariably, this is due to the strength and recognition of the company and its branding devices. Shell, BP, Texaco, ICI, Midland Bank are all examples of companies who have evolved their signs. For example, Texaco (Figure 13), has retained its core elements through all the re-vamps of its corporate mark.

However, when companies need to signal a significant re-orientation of their strategy, or their area of business activity, the logo may need to be significantly amended, otherwise audiences may fail to appreciate the extent of the transformation. For example, Transamerica Corporation had evolved from a financial

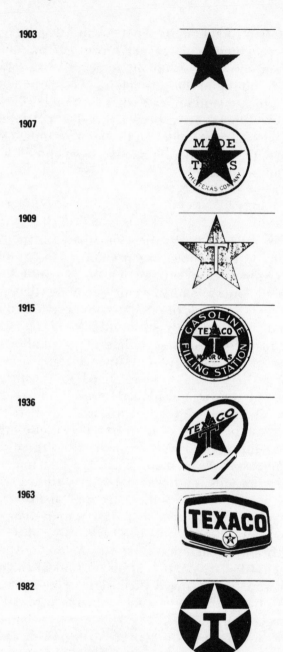

1903

1907

1909

1915

1936

1963

1982

Source: Texaco Inc.

Figure 13   Texaco: evolution of a symbol

services company to a highly diversified conglomerate (when conglomerates were in vogue, back in the 1970s), and back to a focused financial services company in the 1980s. In the process of becoming a more tightly defined company again, various subsidiaries, such as United Artists and Delaval Turbine were sold off. The previous graphic symbol of the company which had become well established during the conglomerate phase, was the Transamerica 'T'. This had good awareness as a corporate symbol, but it was also linked with a diversified company, not a fnancial services organization.

Therefore, to help communicate the renewed financial orientation of the company, a new logo was required. Rather than opting for something purely abstract, the company looked for a relevant symbol. What Transamerica possessed, in its pyramid-shaped corporate headquarters, was one of the ten best-known landmarks in America. The identity consultants decided to evaluate the recognition of the pyramid among key audiences and also to determine its relationship to Transamerica. They found that:

- The pyramid was well known

- It was highly acceptable as a corporate image for a financial services company, but

- It was known primarily as a San Francisco landmark, rather than directly associated with Transamerica.

To ensure that the link with Transamerica would be made now and into the future, the building was registered as a landmark so that the building became 'the Transamerica Pyramid'.

The resultant graphic system uses the pyramid linked to the Transamerica name, which itself is presented in a classical typeface. This is very different to the 'T' symbol which it replaced, and is sufficiently distinctive and noticeable to announce the new corporate direction (Plate 9).

As the Transamerica example demonstrates, logos and consistent graphics can act as unifying devices across a company's activities. This is especially noticeable when a company operates a 'branded' corporate structure. An organization may have decided, for example, that the names of its subsidiaries and brands should be used in consumer markets, but that it also wants to stress the size of its operations to its shareholders, analysts and brokers. By utilizing a graphic as the unifying device on products, brand names can be used to sell products, while the logo communicates the parent's ownership.

This is the approach that the Samaritan Foundation, the third largest non-profit making health provider in the US, uses. The 'face of the Samaritan' unifies all the products, services and facilities whether they are localized or corporate. Compare this new graphic (Plate 10), which is used consistently, with the previous hotchpotch of names and symbols (Plate 11).

The final aspect of any graphic system is that it must be sufficiently versatile to be applied in sizes as diverse as a business card to the side of a truck. It may have to appear with other logos in the corporation, or indeed outside. It may have to appear with and without the name of the organization next to it. It may have to appear in two, three and four colours. A graphic system that cannot meet these criteria will be severely limited. To indicate the requirements of flexibility, the Transamerica symbol had to work in 250 000 individual applications, while the USAir graphics need to work equally well on a lapel badge as on the side of a plane.

Slogans

The limitations of corporate slogans are twofold. First, in an international context they may be difficult to translate into other cultures and other languages. Secondly, most key elements of a design system, such as the logo, the name and the typeface, are planned on the basis of having a shelf-life that stretches into decades. Slogans tend to be more of the 'here and now'. Being specific they tend to encapsulate where the corporation is currently, rather than where it will be in the future. Also, a slogan related to corporate performance runs the risk of becoming negative if the company fails to deliver.

However, having cited the negatives, slogans do seem to have a particular role to play. The communication of a strategy to employees in a consistent and clear way is made that much easier if there is a simple statement of corporate purpose. Thus, ICI's 'World Class' seems to be more about corporate pride, than of relevance to consumer or financial markets, who still undervalue the company. Avis's 'We try harder' was a battle cry for the company's offer, and a motivator to employees. However, Renault Vehicules Industriels, *'en route, ensemble'* may be a valid statement in France, but it does not translate particularly well, nor is it very relevant when there are so few Renault trucks on the road in the UK.

Language

The language a company uses says much about it. 3i, for example, had to work hard to get away from the practice of referring to itself as an institution, as this was totally incompatible with the new, more entrepreneurial direction of the organization. Similarly, companies having determined that they are going to be more approachable, develop a new design system that aims to convey that positioning. They then use technical language or jargon in their corporate literature and a different image is created to the one they desire. Thus, language is as much a part of the corporate identity programmes as design. It certainly has considerable power to define a tone of voice for an organization.

Putting the Elements Together

Although, for the purposes of explanation, the component elements of a design system have been described individually, it is their combination that is important. The inter-relationship of the logo with the corporate typeface and with the style of literature design, is what provides the cohesion necessary for the design system to work. This is where the balance visually between the corporate and the business unit can be resolved. The weight of the two identities can be altered to reduce the corporate at the expense of the unit and vice versa. The balance should be determined solely by the needs of the corporate strategy.

Summary

1. Design is part of the process of communicating the identity, by
   - defining the type of company and what it does;
   - indicating a corporate style;

- differentiating the company from its competitors;
- conveying the logic of the corporate structure;
- communicating change.

2. A design system consists of four elements:
   - names;
   - graphics;
   - slogans;
   - language.

3. Names should not be changed, except as a last resort. It is all too easy to underestimate the time and money it takes to establish a new corporate name.

4. The graphics system can convey a consistent corporate style.

5. Slogans do not always travel well, but they can act as a rallying cry.

6. The tone and quality of language used in communications should not be forgotten. Inaccessible language can undermine what a company is trying to achieve.

7. Although the components of the design system have been analysed independently, it is the way they are put together in a functional and clear way that is important.

References

[1] Matthew Gwyther, 'Anglia Sacrifices its Knight', *Business*, (April 1988)

10

COMMUNICATING THE CORPORATE IDENTITY

'We often say an identity is an empty vessel. It's what you make out of it that counts.' (Jill S Gabbe, Lippincott & Margulies)

Once a company has developed a design system, that system and the positioning statement that generated it need to be communicated to the relevant audiences. If a company fails to communicate what it has done and to support it with the reality of performance, then the process of going through an identity programme will have achieved little; the identity will remain an empty vessel. Indeed, failure to communicate the rationale behind a change in the visual identity can have damaging consequences.

UAL

As a cautionary tale, take the example of UAL. United Airlines had begun life in the 1920s as a US-based airline operator. Over the years, the company had diversified to take in such interests as Hertz Rent-a-Car, Hilton International and Westin Hotels. The move into the hotel business forced the company to adopt a new group name — UAL Inc — as government regulations of the time required United to separate its airline from its other businesses. However, to most observers, the company name of UAL still suggested airlines. With the company planning further non-airline expansion, this was felt to be a problem and a corporate identity review was initiated and a new name was chosen: Allegis. Having chosen Allegis and shed the link at corporate level with United Airlines, the company failed to communicate adequately the rationale for changing the company name. In the end, the stock price went down partly because the loss of the UAL name was not countered by the creation of a strong image for Allegis. Subsequently, the holding company changed its name back to UAL. The argument is a familiar one. Companies have to do more than just perform well, they also have to *signal* that performance and their intentions.

Unisys

A rather more successful approach was that adopted by Unisys. Prior to the merger of Burroughs and Sperry Univac, each of the company's products and each division was different. As Jeanette Lerman of Unisys says: 'We used to look like 10 000 different companies, whereas the market requires us to look like one high quality, consistent, worldwide giant.' To create the necessary cohesion, the company introduced the Unisys name within a consistent graphic style and colour programme of black and red. Unisys was then launched by a consistent advertising campaign throughout the world. Allowing for the vagaries of translating the communication into a variety of languages, the advertisement was the same wherever it appeared. Now, as the campaign has evolved, there has been more scope given to individual countries to tailor the advertising to their needs. However, the logo, the typeface and the corporate colours remain as points of continuity (Plate 12). As an indication of the success of the approach, tracking studies of awareness of Unisys have shown steady increases over this period, while Unisys was one of the winners of *Business Week*'s Excellence in Corporate Advertising Awards, for the best read and best remembered campaigns.

   In spite of the success of Unisys' disciplined approach, most big organizations find it hard to be consistent communicators. The problem is twofold. Firstly, in large organizations there is always some degree of decentralization and devolving of responsibility. This often creates units with their own promotional budgets and priorities. Indeed, they may have their own identities, which could conflict with the overall corporate identity. If these units are geographically dispersed, controlling the communications output will be even harder. A typical example is a multiple retail operation. Normally, there will be a centralized promotions budget under the control of the marketing department. However, there is also likely to be a budget for each individual outlet, controlled at local level to take advantage of opportunities as they arise. Unless the company ensures that adequate controls are in place, disparate messages will start to appear, new logos will be designed and any sense of a unified and cohesive organization will disappear.

Secondly, the sheer scale of some companies makes it difficult for control to be exercised over the sales force and those people who have direct contact with the customer. Nor is this wholly desirable. If the pronouncements of every person within' the company are strictly monitored and controlled, this tends to stifle individual thought and smacks somewhat of Orwell's 'Big Brother'. However, if a large company can communicate its sense of uniqueness and purpose to its employees and a real sense of identity emerges, then individuals will begin to communicate a common set of values. Ubiquity will emerge naturally, rather than being imposed and controlled.

The implication of this, and it applies equally to small companies, is that if a company wants to convey a distinctive corporate style, then it must communicate effectively to all its audiences. Employees will then communicate the style in their direct contacts. The identity becomes self fulfilling. The question this begs is 'How should a company communicate with its many and varied audiences?'.

The Means of Communication

The communications plan should relate back to the identity objectives that have been set. This in turn will be a result of the analysis of the identity and image of an organization. If we have determined that there is a prime requirement to communicate the identity to financial audiences, then this will result in a very different sort of plan from that required for communicating with employees. However, the mechanisms by which a company communicates will broadly be the same, whatever priority is given to the audiences.

Media advertising

Media advertising is one of the more overt forms of communicating a company's position. It has the advantage of being relatively easy to control. However, in large companies there will very often be departmental and subsidiary budgets for advertising, and there is the very obvious danger that messages can start going off in different directions. This will not be so important in a wholly 'branded' identity, but for any organization where a link is made between its component parts, there is the potential for confusion if dissimilar messages are transmitted. This can be heightened if a company has undergone an identity review and is trying to introduce a new name or a new strategic direction. In the period of transition there will often be two forms of branding presented simultaneously. Also this period of transition can be considerable. When BP underwent an identity review it could not change all its petrol stations overnight; nor could British Airways pull all its planes out of service when it changed back to its full name from the abbreviated 'British'. However, the new presentation of the identity is likely to gain rapid recognition and acceptance if media advertising is used to support any change. ICI were very adept at doing this by introducing a major advertising campaign when their new identity was launched. The consistent theme of all activity was to support and endorse their 'World Class' positioning.

The important point about any advertising, whether it be corporate or consumer, is that the overall positioning statement guides the message it conveys. Having gone to the trouble of analysing the identity and image of an organization it would seem foolhardy not to let people know the positioning.

The English National Opera (ENO) provides a good example of this consistency. Everyone at the ENO has a very clear sense of the organization's positioning as an innovative and accessible opera company. This positioning guides the organization in its choice of repertory, in the way opera and ballet is presented, and in the way the company advertises. The company's corporate advertising campaign, based around the theme of 'noted for the company we keep', is a clear endorsement of the company's position, and is aimed as much at employees as at other external audiences.

Literature

Companies of size often produce vast amounts of literature. Where design and production is centrally controlled, it is possible to get a consistency of style. In organizations where several departments generate literature there is the danger that the style and the messages will become inconsistent. Potentially this can create confusion in people's minds, as the picture of the organization that emerges says many different things. However, some companies have begun to control the production of literature more effectively by appointing corporate identity managers with a specific remit to police the visual expression of the corporate identity. Similarly, the corporate identity manual that a company produces in conjunction with the identity consultants, helps in a more disciplined approach to design. This is not to suggest that each piece of literature should slavishly follow a set pattern, but if an organization does want to project a coherent statement about itself, then there should be a commonality of style. One means of achieving this tone is to use a design consultancy on a retained basis.

For example, the publishers Faber and Faber retain the services of the design partnership, Pentagram. Pentagram produce covers for some 200 books a year. The poetry and the play series of books have a distinct look, while individual titles reflect in their covers the content of the work, but also retain in the logo, typography and layout a common Faber look (Plate 13). As Pentagram also provide the designs for the in-store displays, there is a unique look to the Faber product: 'Assembled and displayed in a bookshop, the patterns have a cumulative pictorial effect. They clearly identify the publishers as well as distinguishing their publications and series.'[1]

In addition to creating a consistency of style, an identity review may determine a requirement for new forms of literature or an adaptation of the existing literature. If there is a failure to communicate the strategy to employees, there may be a need for an employee newspaper. Alternatively, if the company's sales force are selling a complex product, then there may be a need for a sales brochure that explains the working of the product. These new forms of literature should be drawn into line with the overall style of communications, in the fulfilment of corporate goals. As with the other forms of communication, a brochure should not be seen as a one-off. It should be seen as part of an integrated approach that makes a statement about an organization.

Personal contacts

Personal contact is one of the most powerful ways of communicating to both internal and external audiences. Within an organization, communications are facilitated by both the informal day-to-day inter-action of individuals, as well as the less regular, more formal meetings of employees through briefing sessions, committees, quality circles and groups. These formalized mechanisms can be used to communicate and make the corporate strategy effective through individual participation.

Kenichi Ohmae believes this emphasis on the individual is at the heart of Japanese success: 'In Japan, the individual employee is utilized to the fullest extent of his or her creative and productive capacity through such participative methods as suggestion boxes, quality circles and value analysis — value engineering contests.'[2]

If this process of internal communication is effective, it will help ensure that employees communicate the identity externally. Again, there are the more informal contacts such as those between the sales force and the buyer, which are difficult to control in any overt way, although IBM have traditionally controlled the appearance of their sales staff through their wearing of dark suits and white shirts: 'For Watson brought from NCR the requirement of the salesmen to be neatly dressed in dark suits and white shirts (a philosophy that has held to the present day): but as a mark of (business) respect for their customers rather than as a uniform.'[3]

More formal contacts with customers through regular meetings or committees are easier to orchestrate and control. However, if those meetings allow free discussion, the real identity will always emerge. This reinforces the view that internal ownership of an identity is the key to ensuring a consistent tone of voice.

Other means of communication

In addition to other forms of promotion, such as direct marketing, PR and sales promotion, all of which can communicate an image of an organization and therefore need to be controlled, all key aspects of the marketing mix have to be considered in the communications plan. Taking the four 'Ps' of Price, Promotion, Place and Product, we should try to ensure that all four components work together to make a consistent statement. These 'Ps' can be defined as follows:

- *Price*   The pricing policy for each product group.

- *Promotion*   The combination of advertising, PR, literature, sales promotion, direct marketing, exhibitions, etc that collectively help communicate an organization's position.

- *Place*   The policies for distributing and selling the product, including after-sales back-up.

- *Product*   The way products are designed, improved, adapted and the way they are presented.

For example, a company should not position itself as a highly exclusive company selling high ticket priced items, only to sell its products in large quantities in discount stores. The price of an item will be one of the clearest signals a consumer has as to the performance of a product. It should signal the positioning of a company relative to competitive products. Of course, as we have seen all along, if the company fails to deliver the anticipated levels of quality for the price charged, the price will have undermined the desired image, rather than endorsed it. A company that has a clear positioning will know what is right. Such is the clarity of Chanel's positioning, for example, that it carefully controls everything it does. Distribution is tightly controlled, the product is consistently presented, and the pricing policy endorses the up-market positioning of the brands.

The Communications Plan

If a new image of an organization is to be created with any degree of cohesion, a communications plan has to be determined at the outset. The relative roles of sales promotion, PR and advertising need to be defined in line with the corporate positioning. And the sort of tracking studies that Unisys used to measure their progress also have to be put in place if the plan is to have accountability. This type of communications activity is a long-term commitment to producing an image that is relevant to the corporate identity and helps the fulfilment of the corporate strategy.

The way to define the communications plan is to use a series of questions.

Why?

Having determined the corporate position, we should determine *why* it needs to be communicated. For example, this could be because there is a lack of awareness as to what the organization does, or perhaps a misplaced image of the organization that needs to be corrected.

Who?

We have seen that a corporate identity programme has a large number of audiences. We now have to determine which are the most important audiences in the achievement of the objectives outlined in the previous question. The audiences need to be prioritized in order of strategic importance.

What?

Although all communication should communicate the desired corporate positioning, there may be subsidiary statements to make. For example, the Royal Opera House tries to communicate its positioning based on artistic excellence throughout everything it does. However, there is also a very specific requirement to communicate to the media and to politicians how the grant it receives is broken down and how it is used.

How?

Having determined what we need to say to whom, the means of communication need to be assessed in order to determine how to do it. The most effective way of doing this to utilize the various elements of the marketing mix, to make a consistent statement about the organization.

When?

Although the communication of the identity should be seen as an all-encompassing and ongoing task, the company still has to determine when to start communicating a new visual identity. The company may determine to do this straightaway, much as ICI and Prudential did, or if the identity review has exposed serious operational weaknesses, the company may decide to put these right before embarking on a communications plan.

How Much?

This final question has no definitive answer. It will depend on the size of company and the complexity of the task. The easiest way for a company to get a feel for the sums of money required is to invite several consultancies to put in proposals. There will likely be a wide variance, not only because of differing fee structures, but because consultancies will view the complexities in different ways.

Summary

1. Although an identity must be communicated to have validity (as both the Unisys and Allegis examples demonstrated), the way in which it is done must be clearly defined.

2. It is likely to involve a great variety of communication mechanisms, all of which need to work together to make a consistent statement about the organization.

3. A communications plan needs to be developed that will reach all important audiences. One of the most important audiences is the employees, for without their endorsement the identity will be cosmetic.

References

[1] Pentagram, *Ideas on Design* (Faber and Faber, 1986).
[2] Kenichi Ohmae, *The Mind of the Strategist* (Penguin, 1983) p 224.
[3] David Mercer, *IBM: How the World's Most Successful Corporation is Managed* (Kogan Page, 1987) p 33.

PART IV
MAKING IT WORK

One of the most difficult phases of a corporate identity programme is its implementation. This is the area where there is the greatest potential for things to go wrong. It is also the area where many identity consultants, having delivered a report and a design system, then leave the client to get on with it. Enlightened clients, or those with experience of identity programmes, may then be able to implement effectively. However, for the inexperienced, it is vitally important that the design consultancy's remit includes the effective implementation of their recommendations.

In Part IV we will look at the process of making the corporate identity programme work. This involves planning, management and evaluation. It also involves the means of creating ownership of the identity and the ways of overcoming the 'political barriers' to change that exist in all organizations. Although a number of examples will be drawn upon to reinforce the points made, two organizations in particular — Unisys and Courtaulds — exemplify good implementation practices. These will be looked at in some depth. The text will also demonstrate that companies need to understand the full implications and pervasiveness of an identity programme, if they are to realize the benefits of having undertaken the process in the first place.

11

IMPLEMENTING AN IDENTITY PROGRAMME

There are two aspects to implementing an identity programme. The first is the practical aspect of planning how and when all the elements of the communication plan should be introduced. The second is concerned with creating a sense of ownership of the identity among the employees of an organization. In this chapter we will deal primarily with the former, while Chapter 12 will look at the ownership issue. The implementation of the visual identity will go through a number of phases, and each of these will be dealt with here:

- Planning
- Launch
- Overcoming resistance to change
- Ongoing management

Implementation Planning

In a small organization, launching the identity programme can be a relatively simple affair. However, in large organizations where there is a large amount of visual communication, often geographically dispersed, and a large number of employees who need to be told about the visual identity, how it works and what it means for them, attention needs to be paid to the process of launching the identity. Large-scale identity programmes can often take years to fully implement.

Take, for example, USAir. To ensure consistency of presentation and the communication of a clear message, the new design system has been applied to all aspects of the airline. This includes aircraft — both exteriors and interiors — all pieces of ground equipment, stationery items, employee uniforms, airport signage, and even coffee cups and napkins. Not surprisingly, the logistics of organizing the application of the corporate colours and new logo to all these items was considerable, and was compounded by the fact that it was not viable to take 50 planes out of service while they were being painted. Everything had to be worked around the flying schedules, so that the minimum disruption was caused to the operational effectiveness of the business.

USAir and companies of a similar scale often phase-in their design systems over time. This has the advantage of being practical, and cost-effective. For example, if a new logo is designed and implemented in one go, it may have considerable impact, but it also means that existing stationery, signage, in fact anything to do with the old corporate logo, has to be discarded. The more gradual approach allows an organization to introduce the new design as existing stocks run out. The danger of this approach is that a company may go through the transitional phase with two contradictory design systems, thus creating more confusion, not less. It also means that when the system is fully implemented there needs to be a concerted communications effort to ensure that the corporate position is clearly understood.

Whichever approach is adopted, a set of priorities needs to be determined. To do this, the implementation plan should look at the following:

● Draw up the list of items that need to be changed and then prioritize the items in terms of their impact against the objectives that have been set. Therefore, if the prime objective is to communicate the corporate positioning to a consumer audience, those items that are likely to have the most impact on consumer perceptions should have priority. Thus, in this instance, advertising, vehicle liveries and staff uniforms would receive a higher priority than invoice design, corporate literature and internal stationery.

	A	B	C	D	E	F
		Design Concepts	Agreed Designs	Artwork Agreed	Items Produced	Launch Dates
1						
2						
3	Stationery					
4	Letterhead					
5	Fax Sheet					
6	PR Paper					
7	Compliment Slips					
8	Stickers					
9	Envelopes					
10	Business Cards					
11	Invoices					
12	Credit Notes					
13	Order Forms					
14						
15	Literature					
16	Annual Report					
17	Corporate Leaflet					
18	Product Leaflet					
19	In house magazine					
20						
21	Signage					
22	Reception					
23	Internal Direction					
24	External Direction					
25	External Corporate					
26	Information signs					
27	Flags					
28						
29	Other					
30	Staff Uniforms					
31	Vehicles: cars					
32	vans					

Figure 14 An example of a work plan

- Once the priorities have been agreed, then a work plan (Figure 14) for every piece of communication should be drawn up. This details when items should be introduced, dates by which they will be designed, when the designs will be agreed, and when the artwork should be complete. As with all plans of this type there should also be included some additional days as a contingency.

- The work plans should then be agreed by all parties involved so that responsibilities are clearly understood.

Inevitably, this ideal is easily undermined. Problems arise when new signage investments need to be made prior to the launch of the new visual identity. The company can either go ahead and use the existing design system and accept that it will only have a short shelf life, or the investment will have to be deferred to coincide with the launch date. Neither solution is ideal. In the case of the former, spending money on a design system that is to be discarded is counter-productive. It sometimes means that a company is supporting a positioning which it will be trying to correct in a few months time. In the case of the latter, it may mean having to make do with something that is inadequate for the task, until the new system is in place. Also, if the particular item is low down on the list of priorities, it may need to be moved to the top for practical reasons, rather than because it is important in fulfilling the communication objectives. Thus, the priority list and consequently the work plan will need to be revised.

The second factor that tends to undermine the logic of the work plans is inter-departmental or inter-business unit rivalry. If it has been decided that one department will have priority implementation of the programme, this may cause dissent among other departments, who may feel that *they* have a case for receiving priority. The lower priority departments may think they are less important or do not have the tools to meet their objectives. If there is an organizational culture that works on the premise that the loudest voice wins, there may be a situation where the priority list is turned on its head in response to internal pressures.

Thus, implementation planning is a fraught area, and a consultancy would be well advised to understand the nature of the organizational culture before embarking on a list of priorities. As with any process of change, the introduction of a new identity system can be traumatic and may cause the emergence of 'tribalism'. This in itself has to be planned for. However, once the plans are agreed, everything will revolve around the agreed launch date. This is the second critical phase in making the identity programme work.

The Launch

The support of senior management, and specifically the CEO, is a vital prerequisite for a successful identity programme. Without the endorsement of the CEO, the corporate identity programme will lack the necessary status within the organization. People will begin to find ways around the system, and communications will break down. To convey the importance of the identity programme, ideally four things should happen:

- Literature needs to be produced in order to launch the identity programme to staff. This should be seen to have come from the Chief Executive and to contain his thoughts. It should explain what the corporate positioning is, how the visual identity works and the rationale behind the programme. To help encourage a sense of involvement, it can include order forms for business cards and other stationery items. The involvement can be further extended by giving employees an item featuring the new design.

  For example, when the Pacific Gas and Electric Company (PG&E), the largest investor-owned utility of its kind in the US, launched its new identity, the company's 40 000 employees received a lapel pin with the new logo and a letter from the President of the company.

- A presentation or a series of employee seminars or workshops on the new identity should be organized. When Prudential Corporation developed their Prudence symbol they undertook a series of presentations to launch their new identity programme to their staff. Similarly USAir worked up one of its planes in the new livery and invited employees to unveiling ceremonies at Washington National Airport, Pittsburgh and

Charlotte. Ed Colodny, Chairman and President of USAir, announced the new look at each location.

- Launch the identity to external audiences. This may involve presentations, advertising and PR. It is important that this takes place after the internal launch and not before, because employees will have to start communicating the identity, and the thinking behind it, in what they say and do.

- Remember that the combination of literature and presentations is only the initial step in the communications process. It will need to be supported on an ongoing basis. Internally, further programmes of change will need to be implemented to ensure that employees understand the importance of the identity programme and to maintain a commitment to it. Also the identity will need to be communicated externally over a period of time. Consistency of presentation needs to be maintained.

Overcoming Resistance to Change

Whatever the strength of support from senior management, barriers to the corporate identity programme can all too easily be thrown up, especially if significant change is implied. For most organizations the process of change is uncomfortable and disruptive. Some companies get around this by building the idea of change into their corporate cultures. Change itself then becomes an accepted part of the way a company operates. However, even in this instance the introduction of external consultants, such as an identity consultant, can be problematical. There are a number of reasons for this which are outlined below.

Using outside consultants

The introduction of external consultants can be seen by employees as an implicit criticism of the things they have done in the past. This creates a degree of nervousness about what the consultant's recommendations will be. For example, if a consultant conducts a visual audit of an organization and concludes that the range of literature is poorly designed, and perhaps even contradictory, then it is implied that all those people who have been involved in its design have not been doing their job as effectively as they might. There may be entirely valid reasons for this, such as a lack of authority in the design department, interference from line managers, or simply a lack of corporate direction. Nonetheless, a potentially confrontational position can emerge, as individuals defend their positions against the criticisms of the consultant.

The criticisms may also involve senior management, perhaps for their lack of emphasis on communications, poor control over resources, or even their leadership styles. Of course, the consultant has the opportunity to water down recommendations or criticisms, so that they are more palatable, but this may undermine their effectiveness. So, if a consultant determines to tell the truth, how is the situation created whereby the recommendations are accepted, rather than 'bottom-drawered' because of their political sensitivity? There can be no categoric answer, as it will depend on the nature of the criticisms and the client/consultant relationship.

However, experience suggests that a relationship where the consultant and client work together to find the answers is more likely to create a solution which can be 'owned' by the client. This is not to suggest that the consultant should be swayed from objectivity and truth, merely that the logic behind the thought process should be shared. This approach is reminiscent of that proposed by Chris Argyris in *Intervention Theory and Method*, in which he asserted that there were three key requirements for intervening in an organization.[1] These can be summarized as follows:

- The consultant should help the client collect valid data about their problems.

- The consultant should not prescribe or impose solutions. The authority of the client should be respected, and the consultant should strive to help people make free, informed choices about their future actions.

- The consultant should operate in a way which helps people to become internally committed to their chosen course of action. Therefore, they will experience ownership of the change.

Although Argyris's work has been criticized by more recent authors, his insight into the client/consultant relationship is valuable because it recasts the problem in terms of building a solution that will survive the consultant's departure. The intervention process devised by Argyris and other organizational development writers is summarized in Figure 15, and shows how identity consultancy can be managed to help overcome the barriers thrown up by members of the organization.

ACTION	CONVENTIONAL MODEL	ORGANIZATIONAL DEVELOPMENT MODEL
Problem Definition	Client	Client ↔ Consultant
Data Gathering	Consultant	Consultant ↔ Client
Data Analysis	Consultant	Consultant ↔ Client
Problem Diagnosis	Consultant	Client ↔ Consultant
Solution Proposed	Consultant	Client ↔ Consultant
Action Plan Design	Consultant ↔ Client	Client ↔ Consultant
Implementation	Client	Consultant ↔ Client
Review	(Client)	Client ↔ Consultant

Figure 15 Intervention methods

Business unit rivalry

In many large organizations, business units have their own distinct histories and strong identities. These units can and do see themselves as different from other parts of a group and different from their parent company. If, as a result of an identity review, the reporting relationships are changed or the name of the business unit is dropped to be replaced by a group name, resentment is likely. Also, a business unit may have built up a strong relationship with its buyers, who have come to expect certain standards of service and quality from it. If another business unit in the group is then given the same name, but it cannot provide the levels of performance, the original unit's image may become tarnished. Michael Porter notes that business units are concerned about this loss of control: 'Business units are concerned that sister units will steal "their" buyers, damage their image or create confusion in buyers' minds over the appropriate point of contact with the firm.'[2]

If an organization has determined to change a branded or diversified identity into a unitary identity, this problem cannot be ignored. It has the potential to undermine the cohesion the identity programme may be seeking to instil. One company manager interviewed for this book proclaimed that his organization's corporate identity programme had been a resounding success in creating a sense of common purpose. All the old individual operating company names had been discarded, and replaced by a more unified naming policy and reporting structure, built around the name of the holding company and the largest product group. Everyone now knew the direction in which they were going.

However, when I attended a meeting of the marketing personnel in the business units, a different picture emerged. In spite of the name change, which had happened some years previously, individual loyalties were still to the business units, rather than to the corporate whole. Secondly, the individual managers deeply resented the loss of their brand names, with their own distinct histories and consumer franchise, for the sake of a parent organization with which they felt no empathy and which had no heritage among their customers. Whether the visual structure that was imposed on this organization was right or wrong is debatable. What was self-evident was that the parent company had singularly failed to create any sense of ownership of the new identity system.

Different benefits

An extension of the argument above is when an identity programme benefits one part of an organization more than another. In some cases, an identity programme, while benefiting one unit, may have an adverse effect on another. To overcome the motivational problems that are likely to ensue in the disadvantaged unit, attention has to be paid to communicating overall group benefits and involving the unit in the development of the group. Communicating the group benefits, and the role of the unit within the group, will not in in itself ensure the commitment of the unit, but it is a necessary pre-condition. The organization will then have to introduce such other elements as bonuses paid on the performance of the group as a whole, inter-unit groups and committees and job rotation.

Ongoing Management

Part of the rationale for corporate identity programmes is to create greater consistency of communication. This can only be achieved by the development of control mechanisms and managers with specific responsibility for communications. Iain Cameron, of the Department of Trade and Industry, supports this point: 'Our studies tell us organizations that are serious about implementing corporate identity do it through strong central control.'

Increasingly large organizations are appointing corporate identity managers to monitor and control the expression of their identities. The other key component of the identity management process is the identity manual which contains all the disciplines a company needs to ensure that after the identity consultants have gone, there will still be consistency of communications. The manual should determine the following:

● What the logo is and how and where it can be used.

● The use of corporate colours (including colour guides for reproduction).

● The acceptable typefaces that can be used in communications.

● The juxtaposition of branding elements on products or corporate divisions/business units.

● The design of external and internal signage.

● The ways and means of laying out letters and documents.

The manual may include additional information dependent on the nature of the company's business. However, the most important requirement of any manual is that it should be simple and easy to use. Some design consultancies manage to produce manuals the size of *War and Peace*. Although a large company may use the corporate logo and colours in a large number of applications, the production of voluminous manuals suggests that either the design system is being poorly explained, or that the design system is too complex in the first place. A 20-page manual would have a greater chance of use and success than a 200-page manual.

For example, the Unisys manual is succinct. It not only explains how the system works, but by a question-and-answer approach it also explains why the typeface has been chosen, how sales litera-ture should be designed, how stationery should be laid out, and how the corporate colours should be used. It is extremely user-friendly, reflecting the company's overall communications stance. Take for example the section of the manual entitled 'Incorrect Uses of the Logotype'. It asks the question: 'Can I use the logotype without the dot?' and provides the following answer:

> Glad you asked. The answer has to be no. And there are several other things you won't be able to do with the Unisys logo.
>
> Why? Because the Unisys logotype is filed as a registered trademark with the United States Patent and Trademark Office. In order to preserve this status, the logotype must never be altered or redrawn in any way. And think about it. Changing a key graphic element of the logo (however good your intentions) might dilute its impact, or detract from the image of consistency we want to project.
>
> Thus we're obliged to impose the following restrictions. Be aware, however, that not every acceptable or unacceptable use of the Unisys logotype can be covered here. If you have any question or doubt at all, contact the Director of Corporate Identity.

When it comes to the visual application of the logo, the manual is equally succinct and provides a series of acceptable colour combinations, and details the ways *not* to use the logotype (Figure 16). The important thing is that the manual never patronizes. It provides explanations as to why things have been designed in a certain way, why certain colours have been chosen, and why certain typefaces are acceptable.

Within any manual there has to be a balance between imposing discipline on the way a company presents itself visually and

*Do not enclose
the logotype in
any shape.*

*Do not letter-
space the
logotype.*

U N İ S Y S

*Do not shape
typography
around the
logotype.*

the full range
of account-
ing functions
to more highly
f e a -
tures **UNİSYS**
s y s -
tems that han-
dle a wider va-
riety of tasks.

*Do not use a
distorted or
out-of-focus
logotype.*

UNİSYS

*Do not use
logotype in a
sentence or
phrase.*

The **UNİSYS** Advantage.

Figure 16 Examples of how *not* to use the logotype from the Unisys
Corporate Identity Standards manual

allowing some freedom to interpret the identity to meet the requirements of a particular piece of communication. If the manual is well thought through, the logic of the design system should present obvious answers to new design problems as they arise.

As companies evolve, problems will arise that had not been envisaged when the manual was devised. One way of overcoming this problem is by extending the range of design options and controls that can be offered by a computerized manual. PG&E have done exactly this by developing a computer-based system. Rather than having a number of people with design manuals making decisions and using their own design studios to put together artwork based on their interpretation of the manual, the manual is kept on a disc and is centralized. Departments can contact head office and make requests for signage or promotional material. The artwork is then formed on the computer to the design specifications laid down in the manual and supplied to the requestor. The computerized approach achieves greater levels of control, ensures that head office always knows what is going on in other offices, and reduces the cost of using external studios for one-off jobs. The overall benefit is an increased consistency of communication. Looking to the future there is the obvious option of introducing inter-active software, thereby making the computerized manual more flexible.

Summary

1. Large-scale programmes can sometimes take literally years to complete. Consequently, the logistics of implementation need to be carefully planned.

2. Companies can either launch the new identity in one go or introduce them over time. The former secures maximum impact, but is expensive. The latter is cost-effective, but potentially confusing.

3. To introduce the new identity a work plan should be drawn up for every piece of communication, with priorities based on strategic needs.

4. The support of senior management, and specifically the CEO, is vital for a successful launch of the identity. The launch programme should also ideally involve seminars or workshops to explain the identity in detail and allow employees to react to the plans.

5. Barriers to change can in part be overcome with an approach that stresses a sharing of responsibilities.

6. To ensure that the discipline in communications is maintained after the consultants disappear, a manual needs to be developed and provided to all those people who generate any form of communication. It needs to achieve a balance between ensuring commitment to a consistent way of presenting the organization and the flexibility to meet new problems.

References

[1] Chris Argyris, *Intervention Theory and Method* (Addison Wesley, 1970)
[2] Michael Porter, *Competitive Advantage*, (The Free Press, 1985) p 387

12

CREATING OWNERSHIP

While in Chapter 11 we were concerned with how to implement the visual aspects of an identity programme, in this chapter we will focus on the means of creating ownership of the substance behind the visual. This is not to deny the importance of creating a design system that employees and other audiences will like and endorse, but it does put the design function into perspective. The true strength of any corporate identity is determined by the acceptance of common values by an organization's employees. Without employee commitment, an identity will lack validity. Employees will simply fail to communicate through their actions and their attitudes the image a company desires, and the more overt forms of communication, such as advertising and PR, will be undermined by what individuals say and do.

The consultant's role in this is quite specific. A consultancy can develop a communications system for a company that endorses the corporate strategy. A consultancy can also support the client in creating ownership of the identity through internal communications. However, at the end of the day, it is the client's management who will create the real sense of purpose, of common values across the organization. As Colin Forbes, a partner in the design consultancy, Pentagram, says about the consultant's ability to influence long-term training:

A nice point to make in a presentation or speech, but what do you actually do about it. Do you take over the personnel department and determine exactly how the company should train people? There has to be an end to the consultant's expertise. You can say training is important, but it's going to be the Chief Executive who appoints the Personnel Director and the people who do the training.

The identity, remembering the original definition in Chapter 1, will be there, whether the company is employing a consultancy or not. Thus, management's role is to support the identity programme with other programmes of change and then to maintain those values and beliefs that are important to competitive success. The organization's role is to continually support and endorse the corporate identity. As Michael Porter says:

There are many opportunities available to senior management to define a larger corporate purpose, to stress the importance of inter-relationships, and to discourage parochial behaviour by business unit, group, and sector managers. A strong set of firmwide values and a strong corporate identity are vital links in reducing cynicism toward committees, resolving conflicts and so on.[1]

The Substance of Identity

Although every organization has an identity, it is the strength of that identity that matters. If an identity programme only involves design it will be a limited exercise. The development of consistency in communications can only be achieved if employees truly 'own' the values necessary to continually support and endorse the identity through their actions. We have seen this with IBM and its strong identity built on widely-held beliefs. We have seen the opposite, where the values are those of the business unit rather than the parent.

Creating and maintaining a strong identity will encompass everything a company does. It will involve, among other things, the nature of the corporate structure, the reporting relationships, the reward system, and the attitude to recruitment and selection. The way these areas are managed will send messages to employees all the time. Therefore, a company has to recognize the communication potential of everything it does. There is little point in developing a plan for the more overt forms of communication and then undermining it, for example, by adopting a contrary plan in recruitment and selection. Managing the identity has to be an all-encompassing process.

Organizations also have to recognize the limitations of an identity programme and have to support it with other programmes of training and change that will help to ensure an organization-wide commitment.

Creating Ownership: Two Case Studies

Of all the companies studied for this book, two stand out as organizations that understand both the power and the limitations of corporate identity programmes. They understand the roles of the consultant and the client company, and they have been able to overcome the barriers to change and create ownership of the identity by supporting the identity programme with other programmes of change.

Unisys

Unisys has been referred to frequently in this book. This is not because of the choice of the name or the design of the logo, but most importantly because the company has a clear understanding of corporate identity. The company defined an explicit role for its identity programme from the start: to develop a name that would help to create a new company, and then to develop a design system that would help to ensure consistency of communication. This was part of the signalling process from senior management. By choosing a name that had no link with either Sperry Univac or Burroughs they were telling employees that neither company would dominate the other in the process of bringing the two organizations together. However, the creation of the new name and logo was no more than a signal and would have lacked substance if the company had not introduced other mechanisms to help achieve their internal goals. These were defined as:

- To estabish one *new* company;
- To combine the best of Burroughs and Sperry Univac's traditions;

12 SIGNS OF TROUBLE

Immediately after the sale is announced ...

1. Pre-occupation. Are people obsessed with the merger and speculation about what it might mean for them? Is this distraction leading to poorer performance on the job?

2. Imagining the Worst. Is your company rife with rumors about the sale? Are people developing worst-case scenarios about what will happen?

3. Stress Reactions. Do people seem tense and anxious? Do you see psychological reactions — fear, aggressiveness, withdrawal — or somatic reations — headaches, sleeplessness, increased smoking?

4. Crisis Management. Is there an air of tension and chaos? Have executives retreated into war rooms and adopted a combat mentality about the merger?

5. Constricted Communication. Are most employees in the dark about what is going on? Are top executives making decisions on their own and restricting contact with the rest of the company?

6. Illusion of Control. Does top management assure people that they have a master plan for the merger, promising that the changes will be handled smoothly and without much pain? Do people doubt the credibility of these promises?

As the companies merge ...

7. Clash of Cultures. Do people see big differences between your company and the other organization and values, or possibly in the style and capability of the two managements?

8. We vs. They. Do people focus upon the differences rather than the similarities between the two companies? Are these perceived differences becoming sharper?

9. Superior vs. Inferior Do people evaluate how your company works in comparision to how the other company operates? Do they see your company culture as superior?

10. Attack and Defend. Are people in your company plotting ways to force the other company to make changes and protect your company from making any? Do they see the other company as doing the same?

11. Win vs. Lose. Are people keeping track of decisions to see which side wins each skirmish? Are some, who see themselves as winners, rushing to impose change? Are others, who feel like losers, revising their résumés and talking to employment recruiters?

12. Miscellaneous. Companies express the merger syndrome in a variety of other ways. In some, people pull together for a common goal; in others, its everybody for themselves. Some move too slowly in the merger, others too fast. Some manage successfully through the merger syndrome. Most do not.

Figure 17   The 12 signs of trouble (*Psychology Today*, October 1986)

● To build a new company based on a meritocracy.

When the merger of the companies was announced, there were people in both companies who felt positively about it and those who felt negatively. As is typical in mergers there was a degree of nervousness about future prospects. To try to create cohesion and help bring the two companies together, one of the first actions was to bring in two merger psychologists, Mitchell Marks of the California School of Professional Psychology and Philip Mirvis of the School of Management, Boston University. They developed a series of seminars for the executives of Burroughs and Sperry Univac. This was an attempt to overcome the 12 signs of trouble that Mirvis and Marks identified in an article in *Psychology Today* (October 1986) (Figure 17). Mirvis and Marks claim that these signs are evident in most mergers, but that they can be managed: 'While they occur to some extent in nearly all corporate combinations, our experience shows that they can be limited and managed effectively with the help of psychological knowledge and techniques.'[2]

A further part of the process in unifying the two companies was the organization of a series of committees. These committees were in effect task forces featuring experts in their specialist areas from both Sperry Univac and Burroughs. Their task was to investigate the operating procedures of the companies, to identify their relative strengths and weaknesses and then jointly recommend what the operating procedure for Unisys should be. As part of the brief was that the new operating procedure had to identify how to eliminate 20–30 per cent of costs, the committee could not simply choose an existing Sperry or Burroughs procedure. Either an adaptation of an existing system had to be developed, or something new had to be created. This meant that whatever the recommendation of the committees, the solution was a Unisys one. Once the committee had completed its work, one 'expert' was appointed to the senior job. The end result of the committees was an approximate split of 50/50 for senior positions between Sperry and Burroughs personnel. Inevitably, the committee stage did not always get things right, but being part of the committee was fundamentally important in fostering a single, unified company with an identity that comprised the best of Burroughs and Sperry.

Finally, the identity and its presentation had to be explained to internal audiences in detail. Mini-courses for marketers and technical groups were organized and the principles and the potential benefits of the communication programme were then outlined both generally, and then specifically, from their point of view. To ensure that the process of inter-action continued, the company then reported back to the groups about the achievements and benefits, both in terms of hard data, such as awareness studies, and anecdotally. The feedback was a further step in the process of fostering a single, unified identity and creating a sense of ownership.

The corporate identity programme was an important element in bringing Sperry Univac and Burroughs together, but what this example shows is that other methods of organizational change have to be used to create corporate-wide values. The various programmes all need to work cohesively together if a new identity is to be created, and they need to be maintained over time to ensure the continued commitment to the corporate body.

Courtaulds

The catalyst for Courtaulds embarking on a corporate identity programme was that with the appointment of Sir Christopher Hogg as Chairman in 1979 the company had been changing its business focus. Gone was the pursuit of growth as a goal in its own right, to be replaced by a concern with excellence of operations and profitability. However, in pursuit of this goal, the visual identity of Courtaulds became fragmented and confused. To signal the change in business focus and restore order to the presentation of Courtaulds and its subsidiaries, a tool was required and found in corporate identity. Roger Myddelton of Courtaulds stated the objectives of the programme in a presentation on the company thus:

1. Behavioural — to use the communications and identity programme to *reinforce* constructive messages about the Courtaulds culture:
   - particularly our commitment to customers; and to ensure businesses are market — not production — led;
   - also, willingness to learn from others;
   - lastly, our ambition to achieve international standards in all aspects of running the business.

2. To bring perceptions about Courtaulds into line with reality, ie:
   - correct the widely held, but unbalanced, picture of Courtaulds as a textile company which had closed a lot of factories;
   - clarify messages about what Courtaulds does and stands for (diversification followed by decentralization had caused a lot of confusion both inside and outside the group);

- raise standards of communication with major audiences (customers and employees).[3]

As with other successful identity programmes, the Courtaulds programme received the full support of the Chairman. Indeed, Sir Christopher Hogg was the main initiator of it. He also saw beyond the purely visual aspects of identity to the need to change employees' attitudes. Only then would the programme have real substance. To achieve this the company decided it would put the onus on its business units. Rather than just imposing change from the centre, Courtaulds' 18 business groups were told about the new logo (known as the 'C' mark) (Plate 14) and what it stood for. As Amanda Haddon-Cave says:

> Christopher Hogg said when he first told them about the 'C' mark, that he wanted it to become a brand that stood for excellence and high standards of performance. The only way that was going to happen was if he was convinced that individual businesses had taken that on board.

Senior management of the business units were then given two years to bring their units up to the required levels of performance. No unit would be allowed to use the 'C' mark until Sir Christopher Hogg was satisfied that they had listened to what their customer and employee expectations were, and that they had acted upon that information by improving communications, both in an overt way and through changing fundamental attitudes among management and staff. To quote Amanda Haddon-Cave again:

> Each of the business groups are required to put together a plan for implementing their identity. That's not just visually. It's what steps they are taking to change attitudes and behaviour and re-focus themselves on their market.

Once the unit was ready and had put forward its plan, Sir Christopher Hogg would visit them and inspect the site and interview various employees. If he was then satisfied with the progress that had been made, the unit would be given authority to adopt the 'C' mark on all communications. The benefit to Courtaulds has been that the individual business units have been highly motivated about the new identity. Courtaulds claim that their approach has created a greater degree of cohesion in the organization, and thereby reduced the number of discordant messages coming from geographically dispersed operations.

Although this method of creating ownership is different from the Unisys example, there is a common thread in both programmes: the management of communications to both internal and external audiences is vital if a strong identity is to evolve. However, communication on its own is insufficient. It has to co-ordinate with other programmes of change to ensure that reality and perceptions work together in meeting corporate goals. Nor does the need to continually reinforce the corporate identity diminish. Both Unisys and Courtaulds have recognized the need to use training programmes to maintain their identities over time.

Summary

1. An identity programme needs to create a common set of values among an organization's employees. Only then will an identity have true substance.

2. The responsibility for creating those values must lie with the client company, who will then have to manage the identity on an on-going basis.

3. An identity programme must be accompanied by other programmes of change, if it is to be effective in creating ownership of the identity.

4. Ownership is vital, if the programme is to move beyond design into all aspects of communication.

5. Unisys and Courtaulds exemplify good practice because they have recognized both the strengths and limitations of corporate identity programmes.

References

[1] Michael Porter, *Competitive Advantage*, (The Free Press, 1985) p 408
[2] Mitchell Lee Marks and Philip Harold Mirvis, 'The Merger Syndrome', *Psychology Today* (October 1986)
[3] Roger Myddelton, 'Using Corporate Identity as a Catalyst for Change', presentation made on 19 January 1988

13

EVALUATING THE IDENTITY PROGRAMME

Given the considerable expense of undertaking a corporate identity programme, there is a perceived need to determine whether the programme has been effective in meeting its objectives. However, although there are ways of gaining an insight into what an identity programme has done for an organization, it is extremely difficult to unequivocally state the direct effect of it. The problem is, of course, to isolate the identity programme from all the other factors that continually impact on an organization and its audiences. Secondly, identity programmes have long-term horizons which create the problem of disassociating the effect of the identity system itself and the management of it over time.

Nonetheless, there are research and assessment methods available, however limited, which can be helpful in evaluating the benefits of going through the process.

Pre and Post Studies

Part of the initial research of an organization's image may include discussion groups or large-scale questionnaires looking at the attitudes of a variety of audiences. This could include such issues as the awareness of an organization and what it does, its size, its structure, the current perception of it and its products, whether staff are helpful, if after-sales service is good, whether prices are competitive, in fact all the details that go to form a picture of an organization (Figure 18).

Topic	Questionnaire	Results
	Recruitment Security question	

The 'Brands'	Awareness of corporate bodies
	  –spontaneous
	  –prompted (level of knowledge)
		–Understanding of levels
		 of corporate identity
		–Competitive context

	Experience of corporations
	  –extent of involvement
	  –immediate impressions of business	

	Perceptions of companies in a competitive context
	  –at a rational level, eg which of these companies …?
	   have a professional attitude
	   are well run
	   are good British company leaders in their field
	  –and on more 'emotional' statements, eg large and impersonal or friendly organizations etc
		–Identification of 'brand'
		 equity
		–Key dimensions that
		 discriminate in the market

The 'Advertising'	Advertising questions
	  –awareness of corporate press/TV advertising
	  –recall of ads, attitudes, communication (spontaneous and prompted)
		–Is my advertising working
		 for my brand and how?

The 'People'	Attitudes to business
	  –agreement/disagreement with statements:
	   I always buy British
	   Large corporations are more efficiently run
	   All large companies should be privatized
		–Segmentation based on
		 attitudes to business/
		 corporations

Figure 18 A broad outline of a corporate questionnaire

Source: Millward Brown

This sort of study should look at the company and its competitors. Quantitative analysis will provide a series of percentages, which can form a point of comparison with the competition and also provide a benchmark for future studies. This is the sort of study that Prudential did which told them that consumers still thought of them as an insurance company, rather than a financial services organization, and like Foremost-McKesson did, which told them that investment analysts saw them as an 'old sleepy company with lacklustre performance'.

Employee research

On different parameters, this is exactly the sort of research a company should also do on a regular basis with its employees. In fact, the very process of doing the research can be useful. This was what happened in the Hawthorne experiments of the 1920s and 1930s, when researchers were trying to understand motivations. Many employees found the very process of being asked questions and of expressing opinions both therapeutic and involving. When Courtaulds undertook the investigation stage of their identity programme, they found that it actually helped to change the culture of the organization from an 'information is power' culture to one where communications became more open. As Amanda Haddon Cave says: 'The main benefit of going through the corporate identity process is that it actually changed the culture in itself.'

Suppliers' and buyers' research

When researching the attitudes of suppliers and buyers there are a number of problems to be overcome. Often the numbers of people involved in buying decisions will be quite small and consequently their attitudes will be surveyed by a number of companies, making them perhaps too familiar with certain types of question. Secondly, because they have a very personal relationship with the company conducting the research, they may be unwilling to express views which might be embarrassing to their positions. To overcome these problems, the researchers should be aware of the limitations at the outset and should seek to reassure respondents of the confidentiality of all information.

However, whether the audience is internal or external, having completed an initial study of attitudes, trend data needs to be built up, such that six months after the launch the same measures can be again researched, and perhaps again on an annual basis thereafter. This accumulated data will help determine whether attitudes are changing in line with the objectives set. Thus, if to help fulfil strategic aims, the key objective of the identity programme was to communicate to customers that the company provided high levels of after-sales service, this should be the key focus of the attitudinal survey. A steady improvement, both against the competition and against pre-identity programme norms would suggest that the programme had been successful. However, herein lies a problem. Which part of the programme was successful? Was it the staff training programme, the communication programme, the design system, or the customer awareness programme? Was it a combination of all of them in equal or unequal parts?

Further research can help us to understand these problems, or strong hints may emanate from the attitudinal study as to which aspects of the identity programme work best, but this sort of analysis can never be wholly exact. The difficulty is that the continual change in market circumstances will impinge on attitudes. In spite of this, studies of this type are an invaluable monitor of the success of an identity programme in meeting its overall objectives.

Communications Research

In addition to assessing overall attitudes towards an organization it is also possible, through both qualitative and quantitative research, to determine attitudes towards key items of communication. This should start prior to the development of the design phase of the identity programme. Existing literature, advertising and promotional material can be diagnosed in research, so that the creative development of the new corporate design can be guided by the findings. This is a valuable exercise and can unearth the sort of confused jargon that creeps into communication.

This happens because:

- Companies lose objectivity over key items of communication. Such is the extent of this that the correction and simplification of inaccessible literature is a sizeable business for many consultancies. For example, a significant part of Lippincott & Margulies programme for Turkiye is Bankasi was in this very area.

- There is a tendency to communicate the way the organization is structured, rather than on the logic of consumer needs. This can be seen in large retail outlets where products are presented in the way the organization buying process is structured, rather than the way that consumers buy.

As the design proposals are developed, research can be used to help refine executions. If failings are established then there is the opportunity to do remedial work. It is far better to spend the money at this stage on getting the principles right than to invest significant sums of money in producing work which could be counterproductive. Finally, the completed creative work and its application to various forms of communication can be tested. This could include the advertising campaign to launch the new identity, a key piece of literature, or a retail environment. Although this kind of research should be treated with caution, as it can become a never-ending task to find the design that communicates exactly the right message, there are still benefits to undertaking it. As Peter Spalding of the research company, Expressions, notes:

> Research can be used to minimize risks after design work has been produced by careful and sensitive monitoring. However, it cannot give you a categoric 'yes' or 'no', as the end product is a creative interpretation and so open to subjectivity.

Sales Analysis

The direct correlation of communications to sales is problematical, because of the large number of factors that impinge on the sales performance. Secondly, although awareness of a company and its products is an important prerequisite in the sales process, cause and effect are difficult to break down.

Having stated this broad caveat, there is one industry in which sales and identity programmes can be effectively related, namely retailing.

If a retail identity, such as that for a fashion retailer or a petrol station, includes the design of the outlet, other factors can be isolated to a large degree. This allows the sales performance to be analysed and the impact of the design to be observed.

For example, when Texaco's US petrol stations were re-designed, the programme included a new logo and colour system, with revised architectural styling and signage. In addition, convenience stores were also introduced at some sites as part of an overall package to attract motorists. Although the introduction of the convenience stores makes the impact of design less clear cut, the result of the programme was a dramatic increase in sales, with the new stations performing better than any of the old stations.

In spite of the immediate impact of a retail identity programme on sales, understanding the long-term effect of design on sales patterns is more difficult. Although other factors can be excluded in the short term, other circumstances, such as localized competition and shopping habits, will change and will impact on sales in time.

Share Price Movements

Some of the companies that were researched for this book had undergone identity programmes aimed primarily or exclusively at financial audiences. These programmes took one of two forms. Either the programme was due to a belief that the company was misunderstood by analysts and investors, or it was due to a belief that the company had not communicated its strategy and its performance effectively enough. A qualitative research project conducted by Margaret Mintz[1] into the attitudes of the financial community confirms the importance of communications in creating a positive image:

A firm's corporate identity is a reflection of management's awareness. A strong management cultivates a corporate identity that conveys an honest picture of its strategy . . . through continuous communication with the City.

Figure 19 Type and number of name changes
Name changes studied in 355 companies. The numbers in parentheses indicate the number of companies studied for each name change.

	Before	After
1. Removal of a limiting descriptor (95)	Hershey Chocolate Corporation Sun Oil Company St Regis Paper Company	Hershey Foods Corporation Sun Company, Inc St Regis Corporation
2. Newly created or selected name (71)	Swift & Co. First National City Corp. American Metal Climax Inc.	Esmark, Inc. Citicorp Amax, Inc.
3. Adoption of initials (41)	Union Twist Drill Company Radio Corporation of America Shoe Corporation of America	UTD Corporation RCA Corporation SCOA Industries, Inc.
4. Simple truncation (eliminating the non-essential) (31)	Ashland Oil & Refining Co. Harris-Intertype Corporation Foremost-McKesson, Inc.	Ashland Oil, Inc. Harris Corporation McKesson Corporation
5. Addition of merger partner, acquirer, or acquisition's name (22)	Phibro Corporation Knight Newspapers Inc. Amerace Corporation	Phibro-Salomon, Inc. Knight-Ridder Newspapers Inc. Amerace Esna Corporation
6. Adoption of an acronym (of the previous name) (14)	National Biscuit Company Continental Oil Company Pepsi-Cola Company	Nabisco, Inc. Conoco, Inc. PepsiCo, Inc.
7. 'Verbal Escalation' (use of presumably more impressive words (12)	Genstar Limited Dun & Bradstreet	Genstar Corporation Dun & Bradstreet Companies, Inc.
8. Change to a descriptive name, or addition to an existing description (12)	SuCrest Corporation Purolator Inc. National Aviation Corporation	Ingredient Technology Corp. Purolator Courier Corp. National Aviation and Technology Corp.
9. Adoption of a brand name as the corporate name (12)	Consolidated Foods Corporation Charter New York Corporation California Packing Corp.	Sara Lee Corporation Irving Bank Corporation Del Monte Corporation

190

10. Adoption of a personal name (11)	A-T-O, Inc. Associated Spring Corp. Saturn Industries, Inc.	Figgie International, Inc. Barnes Group Inc. Tyler Corporation
11. Change of description (10)	Interlake Iron Corporation Mission Equities Corporation Wallace Business Forms, Inc.	Interlake Steel Corporation Mission Insurance Group, Inc. Wallace Computer Services, Inc.
12. Replacement of initials (8)	VWR United Corporation SOS Consolidated Inc. ELT, Inc.	Univar Corporation Core Industries, Inc. Dutch Boy, Inc.
13. Adoption of an acquirer's or an acquisition's name (7)	Lum's Inc. Leasco Corporation Gulf Oil Corporation	Caesars World, Inc. Reliance Group, Inc. Chevron USA, Inc.
14. Legal Status change or similar technicality (5)	M.D.C. Corporation LITCO Corporation Bates Manufacturing Co.	M.D.C. Holdings Inc. LITCO Bancorporation BAV Liquidating Corp.
15. Reversal of an earlier name change (4)	US Plywood-Champion Papers Inc. Acme Markets, Inc. Amerace Esna Corporation	Champion International Corp. American Stores Company Amerace Corporation

Source: Tuck Today

In the US, there have been some attempts to quantify one of the most visible aspects of identity programmes: name changes. (It would be unlikely that this could be measured in the UK, because changing names remains a relative rarity.) Anspach Grossman Portugal commissioned Professors Argenti, Hansen and Neslin from the Tuck School at Dartmouth, US, to investigate the effect of corporate name changes on stock market prices. The conceptual framework they adopted was based on the following:

● A firm changes its name (or proposes such a change).

● The investment community hears about the change.

● The investment community judges the implications of name change.

● Stock price is either affected positively, negatively, or not at all.

The analysis team looked at 15 types of changes (Figure 19) in 355 companies, between 1962 and 1985. The methodology used was an 'event study', which can be defined as follows: 'Event studies are *the* major way in which financial economists examine the effect on security prices of firm specific events and test the informational efficiency of securities markets.'[2]

What the analysts were trying to establish therefore was the additional return created (if there was one), from the imparting of information about the name change. Their findings stated:

The most important finding in our study is that we are now convinced that name change *does* have an effect on stock price. We also believe, however, that the *type* of name change is important, rather than just name change in general. ... To summarize what we found about different types of name change:

1. We discovered effects both before and after WSJ (*Wall Street Journal*) announcements.

2. Effects tend to show up within two weeks of the announcements.

3. Positive effects are much more likely for the following types of name changes:
   - Adoption of acronym;
   - Adoption of initials;
   - Adoption of personal name;
   - Adding name of merger partner/acquisition;
   - Removal of a limiting descriptor;
   - Replacement of initials;
   - Simple truncation;
   - Verbal escalation.

4. Negative effects are rare but were found for:
   - Adoption of a brand name;
   - Adoption of an acquirer's name;
   - Change to description.

5. We found no effect for:
   - Change of description;
   - Legal status change;
   - Newly devised name;
   - Rollback of earlier name change.[3]

In spite of the researchers' conclusion that name changes affect stock prices, it leaves us asking the question, 'Why?'. To this there is no definitive answer. However, we might deduce that the change of name is important because it is a signal of change and of direction. It is in itself a part of the process of communication. Thus, it becomes very difficult to break down cause and effect. However, the real issue in the long term is whether corporate performance and the communication of it to shareholders and analysts meets the expectation created by the name change. If it does not, any short-term increase in value will be undermined.

Ongoing Evaluation

Evaluation is part of the process of ensuring that the identity is effective over time. First, if employees start to become disgruntled, if analysts start to lose interest in the company, and if consumer attitudes start to change, then an organization needs first of all to know that this is happening. Regular and consistent monitoring is the only valid way of achieving this. Once the problem is pinpointed, the company can address the operational and communication problems that caused it. Secondly, it has to be recognized that the identity programme itself is likely to have imperfections, no matter how rigorous the initial research process has been. To ensure that the identity programme evolves and improves over time, communication and attitude tests need to be adopted. Finally, the limitations of the various methods of evaluation mean it is all the more vital, not less, to have as much information as possible built up from several sources and over time. This should involve both quantitative and qualitative measures:

● Quantitative — provides a numerical framework of behaviour and basic attitudes.

● Qualitative — provides in-depth understanding of changing issues raised by quantitative work and acts as an early warning system of new issues that may become relevant in the longer term.

Summary

1. Given the significant investment in corporate identity programmes, evaluation techniques should be used wherever
possible, in spite of their limitations.

2. Pre and post attitude and awareness studies are one of the
most effective means of assessing an identity programme.
However, data needs to be built up over time and against
competitors. Internal studies are also invaluable as a measure
of employee ownership of the identity.

3. Specific communication items can be tested for their effectiveness in sending out the right messages and for their logic.

4. Sales are extremely difficult to correlate with a corporate
identity programme, except in the case of retailing.

5. Work in the US suggests that one aspect of some identity
programmes, the change of name, can impact positively on a
company's share price. However, there is no data to suggest
why this happens and it is also difficult to determine cause and
effect.

6. Evaluation has to be seen as an on-going process.

References

[1] Margaret Mintz, study for Oakley Young on 'The Impact of Corporate
Identity on Financial Audiences' (November, 1989)
[2] Professors Paul Argenti, Robert Hansen, Scott Neslin 'The Name Game: How
Corporate Name Changes Affect Stock Price' *Tuck Today*
[3] *Ibid*

14

CONCLUSION

Although this book is about a discipline that has traditionally been associated with the design industry, it does in some respects take an anti-design stance. This is not to negate the worth of good design as a means of making a company distinctive and of communicating a style or tone that reflects an organization's identity. Rather, it is an attempt to move the whole issue of corporate identity away from the logo or graphic device. When companies launch new logos with descriptions such as 'this suggests the company's new-found technological capabilities' or 'this represents the company going forward into new markets' and the resultant design for both descriptions is a standard typeface accompanied by an upward shooting arrow, these descriptions begin to reek of post-rationalization. Steven Gilliat of Lippincott & Margulies endorses this point:

> There's a lot of people who have a fairly superficial under-standing of corporate identity and the practice of it. They're always talking about, 'these people paid a $1 million for a logo type'. The logo type certainly gets a lot of exposure, but in terms of a professionally developed full programme it is one of the smallest elements.

Of course a typeface or a strong graphic, such as Prudential's or Transamerica's, can suggest what a company is or wishes to become. However, as has been continually stressed, it is the quality of performance and the accumulation of experience, that will transform a sign into a symbol. A logo does not have a value independent of the company it represents. A new logo can suggest a change in direction, but this has to be substantiated. In giving a lecture on corporate identity recently I was asked what Courtaulds 'C' mark was meant to communicate. The answer I gave was that if you find Courtaulds to be efficient and responsive, then the 'C' mark will communicate a well-run company. If Courtaulds never answer your letters or call you back, the 'C' mark suggests a poorly-managed company.

Once the idea of corporate identity as more than just a logo is accepted, we can move identity programmes into the area of total communications. Not forgetting the definitions in Chapter I, the real purpose of an identity programme is to manage corporate communications in such a way as to transmit messages about the identity of an organization in order to create an image that helps fulfil corporate goals. This process involves both internal and external communications. However, the key to a successful identity programme is the creation and maintenance of a common set of values among internal audiences. Employees are the people who, on a daily basis, will support or undermine the overt communications programme. Internal communication of the corporate strategy is thus a vital prerequisite in the process of organizational change. Nonetheless, it is only a prerequisite. It is those organizations who utilize other programmes of change alongside the identity programme that seem to achieve the strongest identities.

We saw this with both Unisys and Courtaulds. The reason for their success is a recognition of both the strengths and the limitations of corporate identity programmes. It is also due to the recognition that values have to be sustained over time and that the identity has to be owned by employees. Without this ownership, change can be resisted. One of the best-known cases of this failure to sustain change is International Harvester's foreman training programme. Here, company foremen were sent to school in Chicago for two weeks of intensive classroom training. The programme was seen to be a success initially, because significant changes in the foremen's attitudes were recorded between the first and last days of the programme. However, further research some time after the programme demonstrated that the positive attitudes had disappeared fairly quickly. As Floyd Mann noted: 'The training did not produce any kind of permanent change in either the attitudes or behaviour of the trained foreman.'[1]

Training and communication programmes are important factors in promoting change, but they need to be supported by experiential learning and by organizational long-term commitment. This puts corporate identity programmes into perspective. An identity programme can signal management will, and it can enable change to occur, but attitude shifts are extremely difficult to achieve and are only really possible through co-ordinated programmes of change.

The implication of the above is twofold. Firstly, companies and consultancies have to work together to plan the process of change. The eventual success of the programme will depend on the strength of the partnership and the ongoing support of the programme over time by management. One of the best examples of this failure is British Rail. In the 1960s when the Design Research Unit (DRU) created the visual identity for British Rail, there was a true sense of carrying the identity right through the organization. However, by the 1980s the failure to invest had led to a visual identity all too closely aligned with organizational reality. The Dutch design historian, Frederique Huygen notes:

> DRU was able to effect the broadest of corporate identity programmes, extending from locomotive to uniform. A colour scheme, the logo of a double arrow, and the lettering designed by Jock Kinneir complete the picture. Over the years, however, both corporate identity and equipment have fallen victim to the ravages of time. Dirty old diesel trains and dilapidated stations are the result.[2]

Secondly, when an identity programme results in the recommendation to change reporting relationships or business unit loyalties, such as when the visual structure of an organization needs to be altered, or when a company name needs to be dropped, serious attention should be paid to the management of change and, in particular, employee motivation. Consultancies should not discard a name, without first ensuring that the reasons for this change are communicated. In turn, senior management need to create mechanisms for ensuring the involvement, much as Unisys did with its task forces, of the divisional staff with the parent organization. It should be remembered that even the highly successful Courtaulds' programme faced problems in changing International Paints' name.

Ten Key Points to Remember

Although there are no easy formulas to ensure that a corporate identity programme is successful, there are some basic rules that help to increase the likelihood of success:

- Take a long-term perspective.
- Set clear and preferably quantified objectives.
- Make sure the Chief Executive and Senior Management are committed to the programme.
- Ensure that any recommendations support the corporate strategy.
- Don't change anything simply for the sake of change. If the current presentation of the identity works, leave it alone.
- Involve employees in the process.
- Pay close attention to implementation.
- Put people and systems in place to ensure disciplines are maintained over time.
- Support identity recommendations with other relevant programmes of change.
- Set up the means to evaluate what you do.

References

[1] F Mann, 'Studying and Creating Change: A Means to Understanding Social Organisation,' *Research in Industrial Human Relations. A Critical Appraisal*, Conrad Arensberg et al (Harper and Bros, New York, 1957)
[2] Frederique Huygen, *British Design, Image and Identity*, (Thames and Hudson, 1989)

BIBLIOGRAPHY

Barthes, Roland *Mythologies*. Paladin, London, 1973.

Bernstein, David *Company Image and Reality: A Critique of Corporate Communications*. Holt, Rinehart and Winston, London, 1986.

de Jong, Cees *et al The Image of a Company*. Architecture, Design and Technology Press, London, 1990.

Deal, Terence and Kennedy, Allen *Corporate Cultures*. Penguin, London, 1988.

French, Wendell L and Bell, Cecil H *Organization Development. Behavioural Science Interventions for Organization Improvement*. Prentice Hall International, New Jersey, 1984.

Gombrich, Sir Ernst *Art and Illusion*. (5th Ed) Phaidon Press, Oxford, 1977.

Handy, Charles B *Understanding Organizations*. (3rd Ed) Penguin, London, 1985.

Huygen, Frederique *British Design: Image and Identity*. Thames and Hudson, London, 1989.

Jenkins, Nicholas *The Business of Image: Visualising the Corporate Message*. Kogan Page, London, 1991.

Kotler, Philip *Marketing Management: Analysis, Planning and Control*. (5th Ed) Prentice Hall International, New Jersey, 1984.

Lorenz, Christopher *The Design Dimension. The New Competitive Weapon for Business*. Basil Blackwell, Oxford, 1987.

Mercer, David *IBM: How the World's Most Successful Corporation is Managed*. Kogan Page, London, 1987.

McDonald, Malcolm H *Marketing Plans*. Heinemann, London, 1984.

Ohmae, Kenichi *The Mind of the Strategist*. Penguin, London, 1983.

Olins, Wally *The Corporate Personality: An Inquiry into the Nature of Corporate Identity*. The Design Council, London, 1978.

Peters, Thomas J and Waterman, Robert H Jr *In Search of Excellence. Lessons from America's Best-Run Companies*. Harper and Row, New York, 1982.

Porter, Michael E *Competitive Strategy: Techniques for Analyzing Industries and Competitors*. The Free Press, New York, 1980.

Porter, Michael E *Competitive Advantage: Creating and Sustaining Superior Performance*. The Free Press, New York, 1985.

Schein, Edgar H *Organizational Culture and Leadership*. Jossey-Bass, London, 1985.

INDEX

wel_terry5872 ②